CULTURES OF THE WORLD
Côte d'Ivoire

Patricia Sheehan and Jacqueline Ong

Marshall Cavendish
Benchmark
New York

PICTURE CREDITS

Cover: © Charles Lenars/CORBIS

Ahmed Ouaba/AFP/Getty Images: 26 • Audrius Tomonis: 135 • B. Vikander/Trip Photographic Library: 10, 90, 91, 108 • Christophe Simon/AFP/Getty Images: 32 • Craig Pershouse/Lonely Planet Images: 1, 62 • Daniel Acker/ Bloomberg/Getty Images: 43 • David Canon/Allsport/Getty Images: 110 • David G. Houser: 64, 71 • Desirey Minkoh/AFP/Getty Images: 111, 123 • Francis Tan: 130 • HBL Network: 8, 53, 103 • Hutchison Library: 15, 19, 50, 68 • Issouf Sanogo/AFP/Getty Images: 23, 46, 105, 106, 109, 114, 129 • James P. Blair/National Geographic Stock: 56, 57 • Kambou Sia/AFP/Getty Images: 28, 33, 35, 38, 61, 79, 81, 83, 92, 93, 117, 118 • Kampbel/AFP/ Getty Images: 127 • Natalie Behring-Chisholm/Getty Images: 82 • North Wind Picture Archives: 18 • Philippe Desmazes/AFP/Getty Images: 25 • photolibrary: 2, 5, 6, 7, 11, 13, 14, 16, 44, 48, 51, 54, 65, 66, 72, 75, 76, 84, 96, 98, 100, 116, 122, 124, 125, 131 • Pius Utomi Ekpei/AFP/Getty Images:40 • Stan Honda/AFP/Getty Images: 41 • Sylvain Grandadam/Getty Images: 74 • Time & Life Pictures/Getty Images: 20 • Topham Picturepoint: 86, 89, 94, 107, 115

PRECEDING PAGE

Two girls on a bicycle in Kong.

Publisher (U.S.): Michelle Bisson
Editors: Deborah Grahame, Stephanie Pee
Copyreader: Daphne Hougham
Designers: Nancy Sabato, Lynn Chin
Cover picture researcher: Connie Gardner
Picture researcher: Thomas Khoo

Marshall Cavendish Benchmark
99 White Plains Road
Tarrytown, NY 10591
Website: www.marshallcavendish.us

© Times Media Private Limited 2000
© Marshall Cavendish International (Asia) Private Limited 2010
All rights reserved. First edition 2000. Second edition 2010.
® "Cultures of the World" is a registered trademark of Times Publishing Limited.

Originated and designed by Times Media Private Limited
An imprint of Marshall Cavendish International (Asia) Private Limited
A member of Times Publishing Limited

Marshall Cavendish is a trademark of Times Publishing Limited.

All Internet sites were correct and accurate at the time of printing. All monetary figures in this publication are in U.S. dollars.

Library of Congress Cataloging-in-Publication Data
Sheehan, Patricia, 1954-
  Côte d'Ivoire / by Patricia Sheehan and Jacqueline Ong. — 2nd ed.
     p. cm. — (Cultures of the world)
  Includes bibliographical references and index.
  Summary: "Provides comprehensive information on the geography, history, wildlife, governmental structure, economy, cultural diversity, peoples, religion, and culture of Côte d'Ivoire"—Provided by publisher.
  ISBN 978-0-7614-4854-9
  1. Côte d'Ivoire—Juvenile literature. I. Ong, Jacqueline. II. Title.
  DT545.22.S54 2010
  966.68—dc22   2009045688

Printed in China
9 8 7 6 5 4 3 2 1

CONTENTS

INTRODUCTION **5**

1. GEOGRAPHY

Landscapes • Rivers • Climate • Flora • Fauna • Principal cities **7**

2. HISTORY

Europeans and the slave trade • French takeover • Wish for independence • Independence and its aftermath • Protests and democracy • The 2002 civil war • The Ouagadougou Political Agreement • The UN Security Council's report on the OPA **17**

3. GOVERNMENT

Local government • Democratic demands • Assembly election results • Military and security forces • Freedom of speech and assembly • Human rights abuse • Wider affiliations • Foreign relations **29**

4. ECONOMY

Devastating debt • Diversifying the economy • Agriculture • Manufacturing • Forestry • Mining • Tourism • Trade • Currency • Infrastructure • Meeting growing energy needs • Working conditions **45**

5. ENVIRONMENT

Forests • Civil war and illegal logging • The Accra Declaration • The Protected Area Project • Pollution crisis **55**

6. IVORIANS

Population characteristics • Indigenous peoples • Minorities • Ivorian character • Social customs • Dress • Social hierarchies **63**

7. LIFESTYLE

Role of the family • Role of women • Children • Ivorian men • Life-cycle events • Standard of living • Urban living • Rural living • Education and literacy • Health services and challenges **73**

8. RELIGION

Islam • Mosques • Christianity • Places of worship • Traditional religions • A blend of the three religions **83**

9. LANGUAGE   Spoken languages • French • Oral traditions • Media   **93**

10. ARTS   Indigenous culture • Masks and statues • Different types of masks • Interweaving masks, music, and dance • Traditional music • Popular music • Traditional dance • Textiles • Jewelry • Literary arts   **99**

11. LEISURE   Traditional games • Storytelling • Sports • Other entertainment   **111**

12. FESTIVALS   Christian holidays • Islamic celebrations • Traditional festivals • Secular holidays   **117**

13. FOOD   Eating styles • Favorite foods • Beverages • Popular eating spots • The food crisis   **123**

MAP OF CÔTE D'IVOIRE   **132**

ABOUT THE ECONOMY   **135**

ABOUT THE CULTURE   **137**

TIME LINE   **138**

GLOSSARY   **140**

FOR FURTHER INFORMATION   **141**

BIBLIOGRAPHY   **142**

INDEX   **143**

INTRODUCTION

THE RÉPUBLIQUE DE CÔTE D'IVOIRE, FORMERLY KNOWN AS THE
Ivory Coast, was given its name in the 15th century by French sailors who
traded for ivory along its coast. A medium-sized country in West Africa, Côte
d'Ivoire became a French colony in 1893 and gained its independence only in 1960.

Côte d'Ivoire has more than 60 ethnic groups, an overflowing immigrant
population, and the highest level of biodiversity in West Africa. It sustains a
relatively diversified agricultural economy, and it is the world's largest producer
of cocoa.

In a region where many political systems are unstable, Côte d'Ivoire had
shown remarkable political stability from its independence until late 1999. It was
conspicuous for its religious and ethnic harmony and its well-developed economy.
A partisan coup d'état in 1999 and the resulting civil war in 2002, however, took a
heavy toll on the economy, with ruinous social outcomes, provoking Côte d'Ivoire
to slip into the kind of internal strife that has plagued many African nations in
recent years.

GEOGRAPHY

An aerial view of Abidjan, Côte d'Ivoire's largest city.

C

ÔTE D'IVOIRE IS SITUATED on the southern coast of West Africa. With an area of 124,504 square miles (322,463 square kilometers), slightly larger than the state of New Mexico, the country shares its borders with Mali and Burkina Faso in the north, Liberia and Guinea on the west, and Ghana on the east.

To the south is the Gulf of Guinea and, beyond it, the Atlantic Ocean. The country's topography consists of coastal lowland, rain forest plateau, and upland savanna.

The beach at Baie des Sirènes.

Despite its relatively small size, Côte d'Ivoire has a wide variety of physical features. The eastern part of the coast is flat and sandy. Beyond the coast there is tropical forest. The western region is extremely rocky and mountainous. Mount Nimba, the tallest mountain in Côte d'Ivoire, is situated there.

LANDSCAPES

On the south of Côte d'Ivoire lies a 320-mile- (515-km-) wide strip of coastal land bordering the Gulf of Guinea. This seafront area is marked by a number of lagoons and sandy beaches.

The southeast and central regions are home to the Baule, Agni, and Abron peoples. The lands around their farms contain the remnants of rain forests that once covered all of southern Côte d'Ivoire. Like much of the rest of West Africa, Côte d'Ivoire has suffered severe deforestation. In 2005 less than 2 percent of the country's land area was still covered in primary forest, and less than a third was forested at all. Agriculture, uncontrolled fires, and logging for tropical woods have been the primary causes of forest loss.

In the north, the land changes to savanna—a large plateau consisting primarily of rolling hills, low-lying vegetation, and scattered trees. Compared with many parts of Africa, the arable land is mostly flat with relatively rich,

Birds gathering along a riverbank in the savanna.

COMOÉ NATIONAL PARK, also called the Komoé, 352 miles (566 km) from the city of Abidjan, is West Africa's largest game park. Tucked in the northeast corner of Côte d'Ivoire, it has an area of about 4,439 square miles (11,497 square km) of savannas, forests, and grasslands. One of the most popular hunting trails during the dry season is along the Comoé River, also Komoé, where most of the game gathers in search of water. Animals found in the Komoé park include elephants, lions, hippopotamuses, leopards, antelopes, colobus and green monkeys, and wild hogs. Over 400 species of birds can be spotted.

TAÏ NATIONAL PARK contains some of the last rain forests in West Africa. The park is about 1,274 square miles (3,300 square km). Trees there grow up to 197 feet (60 m), with massive trunks and huge supporting roots. The tall trees block out the sunlight, preventing dense undergrowth. This primary forest also consists of hanging tropical vines called lianas, torrential streams, and abundant original wildlife.

sandy soil. Such terrain favors the growing of crops, mainly dry rice (rice not grown in flooded paddies), peanuts, and millet.

In the northwest are two mountainous regions, called the Odienné and Man, where several summits rise to more than 5,000 feet (1,524 meters). The highest peak, Mount Nimba, towers over them all at 5,750 feet (1,753 m).

RIVERS

The principal rivers are Sassandra, Bandama, and Comoé. Each river is navigable for only about 40 miles (64 km) of its total length because during the dry season their water levels are extremely low, while during the rainy season it is nearly impossible to navigate through the rapids.

CLIMATE

Côte d'Ivoire has two distinct climatic zones. Along the coast, the weather is humid. Temperatures vary from 72°F (22°C) to 90°F (32°C). In the northern savanna, temperature differences are more extreme. In the summer temperatures can drop to 54°F (12°C) at night and rise above 104°F (40°C) in the day. The northern area has an average annual rainfall of 51 inches (130 centimeters), whereas the average annual rainfall in the southern region is 65 inches (165 cm). From early December to February, strong harmattan winds blow dust and desert sand from the Sahara, reducing visibility in the northern mountain regions.

FLORA

The savanna is covered by low grasses, shrubs, and small deciduous trees. In this arid zone the unusual baobab tree survives by storing water in its trunk, which allows it to get through the dry season. The trunk of the baobab tree can grow to a diameter of 26 feet (8 m), and it can store as much as 31,701 gallons (120,000 liters) of water in its soft wood. In times of drought, the baobab trees are often scraped by elephants that break into the tree trunk to get at its water.

Central and southern Côte d'Ivoire is covered by tropical rain forests with more than 225 species of trees. This area of forest receives an average annual rainfall of more than 43 inches (110 cm). Evergreens and oil palms tower above its dense surface covering of shrubs, ferns, and mosses. There are numerous species of tropical hardwood trees, including *obeche*, mahogany, and iroko (African teak). This area is a great natural resource because the tropical hardwoods are such commercially prized assets.

FAUNA

The animal life in Côte d'Ivoire is similar to that of its next-door neighbor Ghana. Characterized by a great variety of distinctive animals and birds, the country's wildlife is part of the Ethiopian biogeographic zone. Herds of elephants roam the woodlands and grasslands, which are also home to

A hardy baobab tree.

The country has three seasons— November to March is warm and dry; March to May is hot and dry; June to October is hot and wet. July is the wettest of all months.

RAIN FOREST DESTRUCTION

Agriculture provides a livelihood for more than half of Côte d'Ivoire's labor force. The country was once primarily noted for its forest resources. Since the nation gained independence in 1960, however, the forested area has been cut from 39.5 million acres to 24.7 million acres (16 million hectares to 10 million ha). The loss of these rain forests has triggered many environmental problems that have contributed to social unrest and exacerbated poverty across the country. As such, rain forest destruction is of national concern. Today, the Taï National Park is one of the last surviving fragments of the vast primary forest that once stretched across Ghana, Côte d'Ivoire, Liberia, and Sierra Leone. Plants that were thought to be extinct have been rediscovered in the area. Five mammal species of the Taï National Park are also on the International Union for the Conservation of Nature and Natural Resources (IUCN) Red List of Threatened Species. They are the pygmy hippopotamus, the olive colobus monkey, leopards, chimpanzees, and the Jentink's duiker, a species of antelope. Fortunately, the park is surrounded by

a buffer zone that has the legal status of a managed fauna reserve. Agriculture is allowed, but new plantations or any settlements are theoretically prohibited.

About 30 species of trees are of high commercial value. Among the more important types are sipo (utile) and sambu (obeche). Deforestation has increased over the years because of the expansion of the timber industry and agriculture. When coffee and cocoa prices fell in the 1980s, the country concentrated on exporting wood to Europe, its largest trading partner. The government imposed a ban on unprocessed timber exports in 1995, and reforestation began in numerous locations. Illegal logging, accelerating after the start of the civil war in 2002 and continuing in the subsequent years, however, has contributed to the country's having one of the highest deforestation rates in the world. Millions of acres of tropical rain forest have also been destroyed to make room for cocoa and other commodity plantations. Since cacao trees, which produce the beans to make cocoa, deplete the soil's nutrients very quickly, plantation owners are driven time after time to clear virgin forest to take advantage of its fertile soil.

Subsistence farming methods practiced by small-scale farmers also greatly increase the rate of deforestation. Destructive forest fires occur regularly because their extensive slash-and-burn practices leave too many openings in the forest cover.

In order to ship timber from the forests and agricultural produce from the plantations, more roads were built. This heavy intrusion has destroyed many natural habitats, displacing the native animals. When people's food sources are depleted, they, too, are forced to move, following in the tracks of hungry game.

The ultimate results of deforestation are the extinction of plants and animals, the loss of medicinal plants, and an increase in mosquito-borne malaria, changes in rainfall patterns leading to infertile land, and radically altered rural living conditions.

chimpanzees. Carnivores, such as hyenas, jackals, and panthers, live in the same region. There are large numbers of antelope and wild hogs in the country; the most plentiful hog is the red river hog. Manatees, herbivorous water mammals, also live in some rivers.

Lazing crocodiles at the Sacred Lake of Crocodiles.

Most birdlife belongs to Eurasian groups. The guinea fowl is the main game bird. It lives in the forests, is covered with bluish-white spots, and has a red throat and a crest of curly black feathers. In the savanna the blue-bellied roller bird, which has a green beak and feet, is common. The birds are easily spotted on bushes where they search for insects.

Reptiles found in the country include lizards and crocodiles. Pythons and a variety of venomous snakes can also be found. There are many insects, notably mosquitoes, driver ants, termites, locusts, and tsetse flies.

PRINCIPAL CITIES

YAMOUSSOUKRO, also called the Radiant City, has a population of 300,000. Despite being only the fourth most populous city in the country, Yamoussoukro was designated the official capital by former President Félix

The massive Basilica of Our Lady of Peace in Yamoussoukro.

Houphouët-Boigny in 1983. Because of its central location, Yamoussoukro is easily accessible from all parts of the nation, and a high level of commercial activity occurs there. The city's economy is primarily dependent on the timber and perfume industries, and the country's major export crops, cocoa and coffee, are grown near there. In addition, Yamoussoukro's economic fabric includes automobile trade and textiles. Yamoussoukro is also the site of what is claimed to be the world's largest church, the Basilica of Our Lady of Peace.

ABIDJAN was a small fishing village of about 700 inhabitants when it became the terminus of the railroad to the interior in 1904. Nevertheless, with no port facilities growth was slow. In 1934, when Côte d'Ivoire was still a French colony, Abidjan became the capital. It retained this status even after independence because, by then, the French had finished building the Vridi Canal that connected Abidjan's lagoon to the ocean. This instantly gave the city an excellent harbor, and modern port operations commenced soon after. Today, Abidjan is Côte d'Ivoire's main port and largest city. It is the hub of the country's rail and road systems and the center of its cultural and commercial life. It is also home to the national university, several technical colleges, libraries, and an art museum. Even though Yamoussoukro was designated as the nation's capital, most government offices and foreign embassies remain in Abidjan.

The city of Abidjan, intellectual hub of West Africa.

Over the years the population of Abidjan has skyrocketed to more than 3.6 million people, spread over four peninsulas around the lagoon. Known as the Paris of West Africa, Abidjan has a large French population. It also attracts Africans from neighboring countries, making it the region's most cosmopolitan city. Abidjan in the 21st century is characterized by high industrialization and urbanization. It is an attractive and modern city, having skyscrapers—an uncommon sight in West Africa—as well as many parks and wide boulevards, a legacy from the French.

BOUAKÉ is located in central Côte d'Ivoire, where the southern forests meet the savanna. It is the second largest city, with about 1.5 million residents. Bouaké was established as a French military post in the late 1890s and once had served as a major slave market. It is now an important administrative and commercial center. In addition, it is the central market for cocoa, coffee, cotton, yams, and other agricultural products harvested in the region. Bouaké is also the site of a school of forestry and a cotton-textile research institute, and it is renowned for its sprawling market and carnival.

Other urban centers include Man in the west, Korhogo in the north, Bondoukou in the east, and San-Pédro in the southwest. San-Pédro is the second major port and is a center for the exportation of timber and palm oil.

HISTORY

A dilapidated colonial home in Grand Bassam.

CHAPTER 2

INDEPENDENT CLAN KINGDOMS flourished in Côte d'Ivoire for many centuries before Europeans became interested in exploring the African continent.

Unfortunately, very little is known about these kingdoms prior to the arrival of European ships in the 1460s, although it is thought that a Neolithic culture had existed. What is clear, however, is that from as early as the eighth century A.D., Côte d'Ivoire was an important center for the many trade routes that fanned north across the Sahara. Traders exchanged gold, kola nuts, and slaves for cloth, utensils, and salt.

EUROPEANS AND THE SLAVE TRADE

The first sustained European interest in Africa developed in the late 15th century under the tutelage of the prince of Portugal. The Portuguese were motivated by a variety of impulses—a desire for knowledge, a wish to bring Christianity to the pagan people, the search for potential allies against the Muslims, and the hope of finding slaves and lucrative new trade routes.

The Portuguese established a chain of trading settlements along the West African coast. African gold, ivory, foodstuffs, and slaves were exchanged for ironware, firearms, textiles, and European foods. The new trade had radical effects. Previous trade routes had been drawn across the Sahara. When they were redirected to the coast, battles soon flared up among the coastal people for control over trade and access to firearms from Europe. The situation attracted other Europeans who, throughout the 16th century, attempted to take over the existing trade.

Although France was the only country to settle in Côte d'Ivoire, many other countries, such as Portugal, had set foot in the country before France. Côte d'Ivoire has always maintained friendly relations with the West, particularly with France. Its relations with the United States have also been friendly and trustful. Côte d'Ivoire became a member of the United Nations in 1960.

Millions of Africans were sold into slavery, shown yoked in this caravan.

European entrepreneurs were attracted to the country not only because of the ivory and gold trade but also because there was a seemingly endless supply of new slaves.

Fortunately for the inhabitants of Côte d'Ivoire, European slaving and merchant ships preferred trafficking other areas along the coast, such as Sierra Leone and Ghana, as they had better natural harbors.

In 1807, after years of profiting from slave trading, Great Britain moved to abolish it. Their decision led to increased Christian missionary activity in the region. Following on the heels of the missionaries were the European explorers, and their excursions stimulated the interest of merchants searching for new markets.

FRENCH TAKEOVER

France made its first contact with Côte d'Ivoire in 1637 when missionaries arrived in Assinie, near present-day Ghana. It wasn't until the early 19th century, though, that French merchants and their government became interested in Côte d'Ivoire, and they wholeheartedly began to exploit opportunities in the country. With gifts and cash the French government enticed local chiefs in the 1840s to grant French commercial traders a monopoly along the coast in exchange for annual rents and French protection.

The French then built naval bases to keep out other traders. After signing treaties with the coastal chiefs, they moved inland to begin a systematic conquest of the interior. There they met fierce guerrilla resistance from the indigenous peoples and became embroiled in a long war.

Côte d'Ivoire became a French colony in 1893 and part of French West Africa by 1904. French imposition of forced labor and head taxes provoked passionate resistance, especially among the Baule, Anyi, and Abe (Abbey). New revolts broke out when France conscripted thousands of Ivorians to serve with other West African soldiers in World War I. Such defiance continued until 1918, causing the French to become increasingly authoritarian in their efforts to hang on to power.

The French had one goal—to stimulate the production of exports. They planted coffee, cacao, and oil palms along the coast, and changed existing patterns of trade and of political, economic, and religious practices. They built transportation systems so that raw materials could be hauled easily to ports for export. Heavy-handed tax policies were instituted, forcing subsistence farmers to increase their production of cash crops or be swept into migrant labor.

A former colonial resort hotel in Grand Bassam.

Félix Houphouët-Boigny managed to sustain good relations with both West Africa and France.

In other parts of Africa, the French and English were largely colonial bureaucrats who would eventually return to their home countries. Côte d'Ivoire was the only West African country with a sizable population of foreign settlers. As a result, a third of the cacao, coffee, and banana plantations were in the hands of French citizens. The forced labor system, greatly hated by the Africans, became the backbone of the economy. At the time of independence, Côte d'Ivoire was French West Africa's most prosperous country, accounting for over 40 percent of the region's total exports.

WISH FOR INDEPENDENCE

After World War I, concerted efforts toward economic development were made. The French paid greater attention to providing education, health services, development assistance, and the safeguarding of local land rights. Sadly, it was already too late. During the World War II years a nationalist movement began to emerge, and the wish for independence grew. In 1944 a Baule chief, Félix Houphouët-Boigny, founded a union of Ivorian farmers, the African Agricultural Union. This organization had several objectives—to secure better prices for African products, to eliminate practices that benefited only European farm owners, and to abolish forced labor.

From this organization emerged the first major African political party, the Democratic Party of Côte d'Ivoire (PDCI), led by Houphouët-Boigny. The PDCI met with opposition from the French administration because such

such a nationalistic party threatened French control. Tensions escalated into violence in 1949. Fortunately, Houphouët-Boigny had a remarkable ability to reconcile opponents, and this sustained the country's peaceful and prosperous relations with its West African neighbors and with France throughout most of his rule. In light of escalating tensions, he reversed his nationalistic policy and began to cooperate with the French.

On December 4, 1958, Côte d'Ivoire was proclaimed a republic by the French. After the national elections in 1959, Houphouët-Boigny emerged as premier. In 1960, after the French granted independence, the labor leader was elected president. Houphouët-Boigny remained president of Côte d'Ivoire until his death in 1993. Indeed, the nation's contemporary political history is, in fact, closely associated with his career.

INDEPENDENCE AND ITS AFTERMATH

After Houphouët-Boigny became the country's first president, his government gave farmers good prices for their cash crops in order to stimulate production. The focus of development was on methods to improve farming. Coffee production increased significantly, and although it has fallen in export value, it remains a favorite crop and business venture for many families in the southeast. Coffee enjoys a privileged position in the French market because of low production costs and high demand. Cocoa production achieved similar results. Cacao beans became the main export, and its cultivation engages more than one-quarter of the population. By 1979 the country was the world's leading cocoa producer, overtaking Ghana. It also became Africa's leading exporter of pineapples and palm oil. This "Ivorian miracle" was created with the help of French bureaucrats.

In the rest of Africa, Europeans were driven out by the liberated peoples following independence, but in Côte d'Ivoire the foreigners poured in, a result of Houphouët-Boigny's efforts to secure grants of French aid and attract a large number of French business interests. The French community ballooned from 10,000 to 50,000. Most of these newcomers were teachers and advisers.

After a bill proposed by Félix Houphouët-Boigny in 1945 to abolish forced labor was passed into law, the young leader was cast into the limelight in African politics.

After independence Côte d'Ivoire was ruled by a one-party regime. Houphouët-Boigny's Democratic Party was the only legal party, and all members of the executive and legislative branches pledged allegiance to it. A free press did not exist—the only newspapers were government-owned. Opposition parties were outlawed, and freedom of expression, whether spoken or written, was prohibited.

As long as the economy prospered, Ivorians did not complain loudly about the lack of liberties. For 20 years, throughout the 1960s and '70s, the economy maintained an annual growth rate of 10 percent, and the infrequent protests against the president's conservatism never merited military intervention. In 1973, for instance, a conspiracy by army officers was thwarted; in 1980 an attempt on the president's life was made; and in early 1983 student unrest caused the temporary shutdown of the university in Abidjan.

PROTESTS AND DEMOCRACY

Political upheaval and strained foreign relations became increasingly evident from the late 1980s. In 1986 the economic situation worsened. Coffee and cocoa prices dropped, and a world recession followed. Citizens voiced their displeasure with the government, demanded greater respect for human rights, and renewed their interest in a multiparty parliamentary democracy.

Both the external debt and crime in Abidjan increased threefold. The government took measures to restore economic growth, but these makeshift actions were not welcomed by the general public because they failed to improve the standard of living for most people. At the peak of the economic crisis, President Houphouët-Boigny was forced to call in the International Monetary Fund (IMF) for help with debt payment. Hundreds of civil servants went on strike, and students joined in violent street protests, resulting in five student deaths. The unrest was unparalleled in its scale and vigor. An investigating committee concluded that the military was responsible for the deaths, but the government refused to take action. As a result, people began rioting. After months of instability, Houphouët-Boigny was forced to legitimize other political parties, and Côte d'Ivoire's first multiparty elections

In 1995 some 20,000 Ivorians demonstrated for a redefinition of the electoral code.

were held in 1990. Independent newspapers were also allowed to begin publishing divergent views.

Although the 1990 elections were opened to other political parties for the first time, Houphouët-Boigny succeeded in defeating challenger Laurent Gbagbo of the Ivorian Popular Front (FPI) and was elected to his seventh term. He received only 85 percent of the vote, however, instead of his usual 99.9 percent. Houphouët-Boigny died in office in 1993, at the age of 88, and was peacefully replaced by his handpicked successor, the speaker of the National Assembly, Henri Konan-Bédié. Konan-Bédié later won the election of 1995, an election that was boycotted by most of the opposition.

Unlike Houphouët-Boigny—who was very careful to avoid ethnic conflict, leaving access to administrative posts open to immigrants from neighboring countries—Konan-Bédié emphasized the concept of "Ivority." Under Konan-Bédié, the government attempted to rewrite the constitution in a bid to prevent certain challengers who were not of "pure" Ivorian descent from running in presidential elections. This led to ethnic and religious tensions that escalated during his rule. On December 23, 1999, soldiers mutinied, ending three decades of religious and ethnic harmony forged by Houphouët-Boigny and toppling Konan-Bédié. Konan-Bédié fled but not before planting seeds of ethnic discord by trying to stir up xenophobia against Muslim northerners, including his main rival, Alassane Outtara.

Brigadier General Robert Gueï, a former member of Houphouët-Boigny's government, took control of the country the following day. Although Gueï announced that he would allow legislative and presidential elections by October 2000 in which he would not be a candidate, he changed his mind and ran for president. He had also adopted and promoted the theme of xenophobia, banning Ouattara from the election because of his foreign parentage. The 2000 election was a controversial one that saw Gueï attempt to manipulate the outcome. Gueï proclaimed himself president, but he was eventually deposed in a popular uprising that year, and he was replaced by Laurent Gbagbo.

After the 1999 military coup that had opened the door for General Gueï, there were hopes for recovery with a National Reconciliation Forum held in 2001. These hopes were shattered following a failed coup in 2002 in which Gueï was killed.

THE 2002 CIVIL WAR

The failed coup fueled unrest and ignited a civil war, voicing the ongoing discontent of northern Muslims who felt that they were being discriminated against in Ivorian politics. The brief onset of hostilities led to a severe deterioration in socioeconomic and humanitarian conditions. About 700,000 people were displaced and many thousands were killed. The country was pulled apart, with the government retaining control of the south and central regions, and the rebels—called the New Forces—holding on to the north and west areas. Peacekeeping troops from France, the Economic Community of West African States (ECOWAS), and eventually from the United Nations created a buffer zone between the rebels and the government troops.

A rebel leader addresses a crowd in the town of Seguela.

After months of conflict a peace agreement was concluded in 2003, but the cultural and nationalistic issues that caused the civil war, such as land ownership, the basis of nationality, and qualifications for holding office, were never entirely resolved. Despite a Security Council resolution mandating a UN peacekeeping mission with forces supported by the French military, simmering tensions exploded in 2004 when the government violated the cease-fire agreement by bombing rebel-held areas in the north.

In 2005 peace talks held in South Africa led to a new cease-fire agreement between the Ivorian government and the rebels. Both sides agreed to end the war. The terms of the agreement were not immediately implemented, however, and once again the fighting flared up.

Gbagbo's original term as president expired in 2005, but because of a lack of disarmament and the continuation of violence, it was nearly impossible to hold an election. On the basis of a plan worked out by the African Union and endorsed by the UN Security Council, Gbagbo's term was extended for another year. Even though the rebels rejected the possibility of yet another term extension for Gbagbo in 2006, the extension was endorsed by the United Nations once again under its plan to find lasting peace.

THE OUAGADOUGOU POLITICAL AGREEMENT

In 2007, following talks in Burkino Faso, President Laurent Gbagbo and New Forces leader Guillaume Soro announced that they had agreed to a peace agreement aimed at reunifying the country and holding new elections in 2008. The Ouagadougou Political Agreement (OPA) was forged, and it foresaw the inauguration of a new transitional government. Soro was named prime minister. Although the 2008 presidential elections have been postponed several times, the security climate has improved and the fighting has stopped. Moreover, the government has announced that it will hold the long overdue election in early 2010.

THE UN SECURITY COUNCIL'S REPORT ON THE OPA

According to the UN Security Council, a positive political atmosphere has prevailed since the OPA was signed in 2007. While the agreement marks

Participants at a meeting to evaluate the Ouagadougou Political Agreement.

FÉLIX HOUPHOUËT-BOIGNY

Félix Houphouët-Boigny studied medicine before becoming a prosperous cocoa farmer and local chief. In 1944 he turned to politics and formed the country's first agricultural trade union, whose members were African planters. Annoyed that colonial policy favored French plantation owners, the Africans united to recruit migrant workers for their own farms. A year later the French abolished forced labor. Houphouët-Boigny's activities attracted notice, and he was elected to the French Parliament in Paris within a year. He gradually dropped the more radical stance of his youth when he was associated with international Marxist organizations. France rewarded this change by eventually appointing him as the first African to become a minister in a European government.

When Côte d'Ivoire achieved independence, Houphouët-Boigny installed himself in virtual permanent power. He skillfully managed a personality cult by periodically granting amnesty to those in prison for less violent crimes and to political prisoners who had tried to oust him from office. He was a popular figure in Ivorian politics despite his sponsorship of huge expensive building projects in the 1980s, such as the Basilica of Our Lady of Peace, while the country's economy was in a slump. Even after his death in 1993, Félix Houphouët-Boigny is well remembered for the economic and political growth he brought to the country, and he is genuinely mourned by Ivorians to this day.

a major turning point in resolving Côte d'Ivoire's armed conflict, it is only the first step in the right direction. Until the upcoming election, in 2010, all Ivorians need to pull together to ensure that the transitional government effectively fulfills all its obligations listed in the agreement. Although it calls for Ivorian parties to make tangible progress toward lasting peace, the UN secretary-general has expressed deep concern at the failure of the principal players to adhere to the time lines set out in the document. More needs to be done because, despite improved security measures, the overall peace process remains quite fragile. Concrete progress needs to be made particularly in the dismantling of militias, disarmament of combatants, identification of the population, restoration of state authority throughout the country, unification of the two armed forces, and official sanction for human rights.

GOVERNMENT

The chamber of the National Assembly in Abidjan.

CHAPTER 3

FROM INDEPENDENCE TO 1990 Côte d'Ivoire had a one-party government. All candidates for the National Assembly belonged to the PDCI, which was considered the only legal party. In 1990, however, other parties were legalized. Today Côte d'Ivoire is a multiparty republic with an independent judiciary and national legislature. More than 100 political parties have been established.

LOCAL GOVERNMENT

Côte d'Ivoire is divided into 19 regions, each ruled by a regional governor nominated by the Ministry of Interior and appointed by the president. These regions are further divided into 90 departments, and every region and department is led by a prefect appointed by the central government. In 2002 the country held its first elections to select departmental councils whose task is to oversee local organizational development, and as well to support economic and social planning and projects. The departments are divided into 190 communes, each headed by an elected mayor.

DEMOCRATIC DEMANDS

The Ivorian constitution affords the legislature some independence, but it has not often been exercised. Until 1995 the PDCI maintained

POLITICAL STRUCTURE

EXECUTIVE POWER is personified in the president, who is elected for a five-year term. The president of Côte d'Ivoire is the head of state and commander in chief of the armed forces. The president appoints a prime minister as head of his government. The prime minister, in turn, appoints a ministerial cabinet to carry out the work of the government.

Veteran politician Laurent Gbagbo was elected president in 2000 for a five-year term of office, and was awarded a seventh successive year in power in November 2006 under a UN plan to find lasting peace. A new transitional government, formed in 2007 and led by President Gbagbo, is currently in power, and elections are scheduled to take place in November 2010.

JUDICIAL POWER is based on French civil law, with the highest level of authority in the hands of the supreme court. A high court of justice has the authority to try government officials, even the president. Lower courts include the appellate, or court of appeals, state security, and court of first instance (an initial trial court). There is also an independent Constitutional Council consisting of seven members appointed by the president. This council is responsible for determining the eligibility of candidates running in presidential and legislative elections, the announcement of final election results, the conduct of referendums, and the constitutionality of legislation.

LEGISLATIVE POWER is exercised by the National Assembly, which is run like a parliament. Its 225 members are elected by direct popular vote to serve five-year terms concurrently with the president. It passes on legislation typically introduced by the president, but it can also introduce legislation.

its political dominance despite multiparty presidential and legislative elections in 1990. In October 1995 major opposition parties boycotted the presidential election, citing irregularities in the electoral code and voter registration. They claimed that the government used the 1994 electoral code to place formidable obstacles in the path of political rivals. One of

ELECTORAL SYSTEM

Number of constituencies

225 constituencies

Voting system

- *Simple majority vote in one round.*
- *Vacancies arising between general elections are filled by by-elections held within three months. No by-election is held within the last 12 months of a legislative term.*
- *Voting is not compulsory.*

Voter requirements

- *Age: 21 years.*
- *Côte d'Ivoire citizenship.*
- *Full possession of civil and political rights.*
- *Disqualifications: insanity, conviction for crime.*

Candidate eligibility

- *Age: 23 years.*
- *Côte d'Ivoire citizenship.*
- *Ineligibility: guardianship, work undertaken for and financed by a foreign state or international organization, executive in a national enterprise, or one benefiting from state concessions.*

the opposition parties, the Rally of Republicans (RDR), held that Alassane Ouattara, a leading rival to Henri Konan-Bédié, had been unfairly excluded from entering the presidential race. The opposition also complained that there were not enough checks to ensure that prospective voters were eligible. They denounced restrictions on marches and sit-ins three months prior to the election, which had been an attempt to guarantee public order. The opposition called for an active boycott of the presidential election. They blocked access to polling stations and prevented delivery of election materials. Talks between the government and opposition groups broke down over this issue, despite concessions on both sides. The dispute left at least five people dead.

In early November 1995 negotiations between the government and the opposition parties led to an agreement in which the controversial electoral lists would be revised. As a result, the boycott was lifted and nine opposition parties challenged the ruling PDCI for the 175 parliamentary seats. A number of independent candidates, some of whom had left the PDCI, also joined the race.

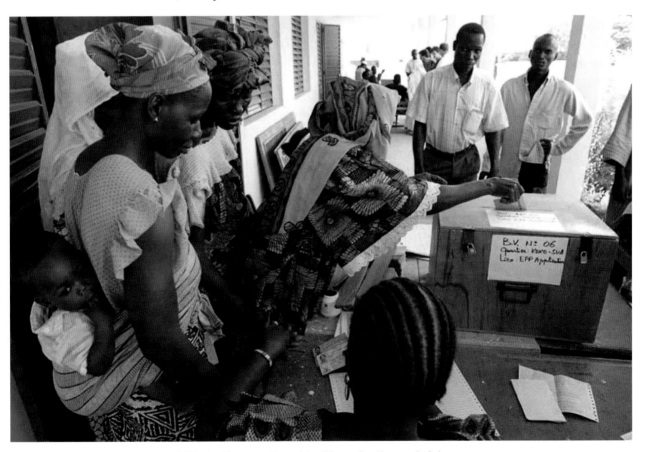

The 1995 election was fraught with contention and violence.

Pro-government police patrolling the streets in the wake of violent clashes over impending elections in 2006.

ASSEMBLY ELECTION RESULTS

Despite these negotiations and changes, the most recent National Assembly election, held in December 2000, once again plunged Côte d'Ivoire into chaos. It was marred by violence, irregularities, and a low participation rate of 33 percent. At least 40 people were killed in Abidjan alone. The continued RDR boycott in protest of the invalidation of the candidacy of party president Alassane Ouattara was largely to blame for the low participation. In addition, the election could not be held in 26 electoral districts in the north because RDR activists had disrupted polling stations, burned ballots, and threatened the safety of election officials. A legislative by-election was held in January 2001, in which 223 of the 225 seats were filled. President Laurent Gbagbo's party, the FPI, held 96 seats; the PDCI 94 seats; four militants from the Workers' Party of Côte d'Ivoire (PTI) took 4 seats; and independent candidates and very small parties held 2 and 22 seats, respectively. In spite of its boycott of the legislative election, the RDR won 5 seats.

"When a regime is bad, we have to combat it with whatever means possible in order to achieve change and remove dictators."
—Laurent Gbagbo, leader of the FPI and president of Côte d'Ivoire

Following the disordered 2000 National Assembly election that left at least 40 people dead, Amnesty International reported that human rights violations and serious disturbances arose principally from conflict between members and sympathizers of two opposing political parties, Ouattara's RDR and Gbagbo's FPI. The global organization demanded that those in charge of security forces move to protect the human rights of the whole population, including foreign nationals who have been targeted by other civilians or even by certain members of the security forces. According to Amnesty International, security forces had in some cases joined FPI supporters in street fighting against members of the RDR. In other cases gendarmerie—national police—protected members of the RDR who had been threatened with lynching. Hence, Amnesty International implored all political officeholders, particularly Gbagbo and Outtara, to urge their supporters to respect human rights. The organization claimed that the threat of civil war still hung over Côte d'Ivoire and recommended that all political, military, and religious leaders join together to dispel the cloud of ethnic and religious divisions that would inevitably lead to bolder human rights violations. It is important to note that Amnesty International does not favor any particular type of government but insists that those in power respect human rights universally, including the right to life and absolute freedom from torture.

MILITARY AND SECURITY FORCES

Since the outbreak of violence in September 2002 that split the country, the nation's military has undergone restructuring. The former system that broke the country into four military regions no longer exists. The more than 30,000-strong Ivorian Defense and Security Forces (FDS) include the army, navy, air force, gendarmerie, police, and other paramilitary forces.

The headquarters of the Ivorian National Armed Forces (FANCI) is in Abidjan, and it is commanded by a major general. The gendarmerie, consisting of 12,000 men, is also commanded by a major general. It is a national police force responsible for territorial security especially in the rural areas. The gendarmes are also deployed in times of national crisis to reinforce the army.

Côte d'Ivoire has a brown-water navy for coastal surveillance and security for the nation's 320-mile (515-km) coastline. The operational capability of the navy's vessels has degraded since the war began, and the navy is unable to carry out its missions beyond the general area of Abidjan.

The Ivorian air force's function is to defend the nation's airspace. In addition, it provides transportation support to other services. At present the air force has two presidential jets, one transport or utility aircraft that is not regularly used, one utility helicopter, and one attack helicopter.

In 1961 France and Côte d'Ivoire signed a mutual defense accord providing for the stationing of French forces in Côte d'Ivoire. Shortly after the start of the hostilities in 2002, France deployed troops primarily to

The army is the largest branch of the armed forces. Paramilitary forces include a presidential guard and the gendarmerie (national police force).

Troops being reviewed before deployment to a rebel stronghold in northern Côte d'Ivoire.

protect French nationals, but this move also aided Ivorian forces. In January 2003 the ECOWAS also placed about 1,500 peacekeeping troops from five countries. These troops later became part of the UN Operation in Côte d'Ivoire (UNOCI). Since then, especially after the signing of the Ouagadougou Political Agreement (OPA) in 2007, the number of such troops has fallen in light of the progress the Ivorians have made. The UN Security Council Resolution has continued to extend the mandate, the latest one ending on January 31, 2010.

FREEDOM OF SPEECH AND ASSEMBLY

Although the constitution provides for freedom of expression, in reality this liberty is still restricted. The government does not tolerate what it considers insults or attacks on the honor or dignity of the country's highest officials, and such offenses are punishable by prison sentences. Some teachers who are involved in opposition politics report that they have been transferred because of their political activities. In fact, the Paris-based media watchdog Reporters Without Borders considers Côte d'Ivoire as "one of Africa's most dangerous countries for both local and foreign media." There is no doubt, however, that political discourse today is considerably freer than it was before 1990. Opposition parties and independent newspapers as well as independent trade unions were made legal in 1990. The opposition press also frequently prints its criticism of the government.

The constitution also provides for freedom of assembly. In practice that freedom is limited whenever the government perceives a danger to public order. Groups wishing to hold demonstrations or rallies must submit a notice to either the Ministry of Security or Ministry of Interior 48 hours before the proposed event. The government sometimes denies permission to the opposition to assemble in outdoor public locations. Following opposition demonstrations in September 1995, the government announced that all marches and sit-ins were to be banned for a three-month period in all streets and public places. The decree was selectively applied—only opposition events were affected. Penalties for infractions ranged from no action to 12 months' imprisonment. An "antivandalism" law, passed by the National Assembly in 1992, holds organizers of a march or demonstration responsible if any of the participants engage in violence.

In 1991 the government banned the previously registered student union FESCI after a student was killed by other students, but FESCI remains active in demonstrations, ceremonies, and political party conventions. In December 1996 the police broke up an informal memorial service organized by students and held on the university campus. On December 19, four FESCI leaders who appeared at the office of the Minister of Security—at the minister's invitation, they said—were arrested. On January 7, 1997, three of the four students were convicted and sentenced to two years in prison under the "antivandalism" law and laws against disturbing the public order.

HUMAN RIGHTS ABUSE

The government has cooperated with international inquiries into its human rights practices, but various human rights organizations have alleged that although there has been some improvement, particularly after the signing of the 2007 Ouagadougou Agreement, serious abuses persist. The judiciary, theoretically independent, is subject to executive branch pressure and does not always ensure due process of law.

The United Nations asserts that the prevailing human rights situation in Côte d'Ivoire continues to be characterized by abuses inflicted on civilians by the government's defense and security forces. Intimidation, arbitrary arrest and detention, and racketeering continue to occur at checkpoints. With a high rate of violent civil crimes, security forces are said to exert a shoot-to-kill policy when pursuing criminal suspects. Official corruption is also rampant in Côte d'Ivoire.

Cases of abuse of women and children have been recorded, with reports of discrimination and violence against women, including female circumcision and child molestation. Human trafficking—including children for forced labor, prostitution, and armed assault—is also a growing problem in Côte d'Ivoire.

In 2007 the U.S. Congress introduced the Child Soldier Prevention Act that is crafted to encourage governments around the world to disarm, demobilize, and rehabilitate child soldiers from government forces and government-supported militias.

A banner encouraging Ivorian women to say no to assault and battery at home.

The national Human Rights Commission, established in January 2007, has been collaborating closely with the UNOCI to promote and defend human rights. As Côte d'Ivoire emerges from conflict, the new commission is expected to help bolster human rights by integrating a humanistic overview into the various planning processes of the United Nations. It has so far established good partnerships with state authorities, particularly the Ministries of Justice and Human Rights, Interior, Defense and Communication as well as with civil society in general. The commission has coordinated with the Ministry of Justice and Human Rights, and it has cooperated with countrywide nongovernmental organizations (NGOs) to set up more than 70 human rights clubs in primary and secondary schools.

CÔTE D'IVOIRE'S WOMEN AND CHILDREN

DOMESTIC VIOLENCE *The legal code in Côte d'Ivoire does not define domestic violence, which is a serious problem in the country. Female victims of domestic violence suffer severe social stigmatization and, as a result, often will not report or discuss domestic violence. Domestic violence in Côte d'Ivoire is considered an issue to be addressed within the family unless serious bodily harm is inflicted or if the victim files a complaint. Police often ignore reports of violence and rape, while women's advocacy groups continue to protest the indifference of authorities to such crimes. These groups, such as the Association of Women Lawyers, also continue to sponsor campaigns against the ongoing issues of forced marriages, marriage of minors, and practices that are considered harmful to women and girls. Even though the law prohibits forced marriages, they still take place throughout the country. The law specifically penalizes anyone who forces a minor under the age of 18 to enter a religious or traditional matrimonial union. Unfortunately, tribal marriages are commonly performed with girls as young as 14, particularly in the north.*

CHILD LABOR *Child labor is another major problem in Côte d'Ivoire. In 2003, 20 percent of children below the 10 to 14 age-group in Côte d'Ivoire were working full time, exposing them to domestic and sexual abuse. As a result of the civil war and the political crisis that followed it, many families were displaced, and children were increasingly relied on to provide for their families. Women and children are also being trafficked from Côte d'Ivoire to other African countries, Europe, and the Middle East for prostitution and sexual exploitation as well as agricultural and domestic labor.*

CHILD SOLDIERS *Human Rights Watch reports that Ivorian forces have been recruiting hundreds of children as soldiers, sex slaves, spies, and even human shields. Children as young as 13 are crossing the western borders between Côte d'Ivoire and Liberia to join militias supporting President Gbagbo, although it is considered a war crime to recruit children younger than 15. While some of these children voluntarily enlist in the army in return for food, clothing, and shelter, there are reports of children being kidnapped from schools or their homes. Once recruited, many of these boy soldiers are brainwashed, trained, given drugs, and then sent into the battlefield with firearms and orders to kill. As a result, their lives and health are squandered and their childhoods are sacrificed.*

Leaders of the West African nations after an **ECOWAS** meeting in 2009.

WIDER AFFILIATIONS

The Ivorian government in the past has acted as mediator in conflicts in other countries of Africa. In 1997 President Henri Bédié met with the Angolan leader, Jonas Savimbi, to encourage him to cooperate with the United Nations in the implementation of the Angola peace process. President Bédié also visited South Africa in 1998 at the invitation of President Nelson Mandela. The aim was to consolidate existing trade and economic relations between the two countries, which are two of the larger economies in Africa. Bédié's visit to the widely praised leader was depicted by the Ivorian official press as a sign of the changing political climate in Africa as a whole.

Côte d'Ivoire is a member of the Economic Community of West African States and supports that organization's efforts to have a regional military force as a future peacekeeping body. ECOWAS and the Organization of

African Unity (OAU), a political organization that aims to promote unity among African countries, improve living standards in them all, and establish international cooperation, are both robustly supported by the majority of Ivorians. These hands-on groups are viewed as successful in providing a framework for African nations to cooperate with each other in promoting peace and democracy.

FOREIGN RELATIONS

There is no doubt that Côte d'Ivoire has played an important and constructive role in the region and has maintained close ties with its African counterparts. Looking beyond the borders, Côte d'Ivoire also has a foreign policy that is favorable to the West and has been a member of the United Nations since independence in 1960. It has participated in

Côte d'Ivoire's minister of foreign affairs, Youssouf Bakayoko, speaking at the United Nations.

most of the UN's specialized agencies, including the African Union, West African Economic and Monetary Union, and ECOWAS. It also belongs to the European Investment Bank and the African Development Bank. It is an associate member of the European Union.

Even though Côte d'Ivoire's foreign policy maintains a variety of diplomatic contacts, France has always been the nation's single most important foreign partner. Former President Houphouët-Boigny was a minister in the French government before Côte d'Ivoire's independence, and he had insisted that the country's relationship with France remain strong. Gallic influences are seen everywhere in Côte d'Ivoire. For instance, French is Côte d'Ivoire's official language, the country has adopted the French legal system, and thousands of French expatriates work their entire careers in Côte d'Ivoire. Bilateral relations between the two nations continue to improve amid ongoing French military and diplomatic efforts to promote peace and stability in Côte d'Ivoire.

Côte d'Ivoire also maintains a sound relationship with the United States, although an undeniable strain between the two resulted from restrictions on nonhumanitarian aid imposed on the African nation following the December 1999 coup d'état. The United States participates in the international effort to assist Côte d'Ivoire in its current political crisis and has provided the country with more than a quarter of the funding for the ongoing UN peacekeeping mission. The United States has also provided economic support fund assistance to promote democracy. It is sympathetic, too, to the country's desire for a quick and orderly economic development agenda. Côte d'Ivoire is a major beneficiary of U.S. assistance in combating HIV/AIDS, and it is one of the 15 countries under the President's Emergency Plan for AIDS Relief.

Apart from financial aid, the United States and Côte d'Ivoire conduct an active cultural exchange program, which enables prominent Ivorian government officials, civic leaders, media representatives, educators, artists, and scholars to visit the United States, better acquainting them with the American people. These visits facilitate an exchange of ideas and views.

Laurent Gbagbo was born in 1945 to a Roman Catholic family of the Bete people in the village of Mama near Gagnoa. He moved to the capital city in the 1960s and attended the Traditional College of Abidjan in 1965. Gbagbo then studied history at the University of Abidjan and continued his studies at the Sorbonne in Paris. Gbagbo later returned to Côte d'Ivoire to teach in the Classical College.

A historian by profession, President Gbagbo is also a former trade union activist who has demonstrated a strong nationalist stance since the 1980s, espousing the concept of pure Ivorian parentage in electoral eligibility. He was a vocal opponent of the regime of former President Houphouët-Boigny. Gbagbo spent the early 1970s in prison for subversive teaching and eight years in exile in France in the 1980s for forming an opposition group. When he returned in 1988 to campaign for multiparty democracy, he was elected to lead the FPI. Two years later then President Houphouët-Boigny agreed to recognize opposition parties, and for the first time in the nation's history, multiparty elections were scheduled.

Even though Houphouët-Boigny won the 1990 elections, Gbagbo resumed his political activism and endured another prison sentence, this time for organizing a student protest in 1992.

Laurent Gbagbo was elected president in 2000 for a five-year mandate and later a successive seventh year in power amid an uprising against his predecessor, Brigadier General Robert Gueï. Almost immediately after Gbagbo took office, rebel forces revolted, igniting a civil war in 2002. The French assisted in brokering a peace agreement between the government and rebel forces in 2003, and the war was declared ended in July the same year. Although the country remains fragmented, Gbagbo and rebel forces' young commander Guillaume Soro signed a power-sharing deal in 2007. Soro became the country's prime minister, while Gbagbo remained president.

ECONOMY

Ivorian workers at a cotton factory.

THE ECONOMY OF CÔTE D'IVOIRE relies primarily on agriculture. It had a good financial reputation for many years, but this began to change in the 1980s. The country experienced seven years of recession from 1987 to 1993, and from September 2008 onward there was a significant fall in the world prices of cocoa and coffee—Côte d'Ivoire's two leading agricultural exports.

Political instability since the late 1990s has itself taken a heavy toll on economic growth and widened poverty. The division of the country disrupted trade and diminished Côte d'Ivoire's role as a regional hub. This led to a fall in export growth. Foreign direct investments also took a major hit, and while waiting for a resolution of the crisis, many foreign companies closed and went home or scaled down their operations. Although Côte d'Ivoire is still dealing with the consequences of the political crisis and remains deep in debt, its economy is actually on the road to recovery as the political situation returns to normal.

DEVASTATING DEBT

Most African countries do not have the spending money to develop their economies. Foreign private enterprise has often considered investment in these underdeveloped areas too risky. Thus the major

Prime minister of Cote d'Ivoire, Guillaume Soro (*right*), welcoming IMF representative Arend Kouwenaar.

alternative sources of financing are national and multinational lending institutions such as the World Bank and the IMF. In 2008 the World Bank announced that Côte d'Ivoire had fully paid its arrears, paving the way for new assistance. In the following year the IMF agreed to lend Côte d'Ivoire $565 million. Attached to the loan were strict conditions relating to poverty reduction and financial transparency that Côte d'Ivoire had to adhere to. Côte d'Ivoire's national debt stands at $12.8 billion; but in March 2009 the World Bank's International Development Association (IDA) and the IMF agreed that Côte d'Ivoire qualified for debt relief under the enhanced Heavily Indebted Poor Countries (HIPC) initiative. This means that Côte d'Ivoire will receive interim debt relief from certain creditors. In order to qualify for such relief, however, Côte d'Ivoire would have to implement a broad set of reforms.

Côte d'Ivoire has done this by adopting a Poverty Reduction Strategy (PRS) and establishing a track record of policy performance under the economic programs supported by the IMF's Emergency Post-Conflict Assistance. Côte d'Ivoire has to implement PRS for at least one year, and at the same time continue to maintain macroeconomic stability.

Things are starting to look up for Côte d'Ivoire. The IMF has agreed to write off the nation's $3 billion debt. In addition, the Paris Club of creditors agreed to defer collections until April 2012 on some of its outstanding loans that are overdue. The deal is expected to reduce debt repayments to the club from $4.6 billion to $391 million.

DIVERSIFYING THE ECONOMY

The economy is largely market-based, and it depends heavily on the agricultural sector. Almost 70 percent of the people living in Côte d'Ivoire

Both the International Monetary Fund (IMF) and the World Bank (WB) are owned and directed by the governments of member nations. The IMF is led by a board of governors that is advised by two ministerial committees, the International Monetary and Financial Committee (IMFC) and the Development Committee. The World Bank on the other hand is led by an elected president and consists of two development institutions, the International Bank for Reconstruction and Development (IBRD) and the International Development Association (IDA). The IMF lends money when member countries, typically developing ones, encounter balance-of-payments problems. Accepting a loan means big internal economic changes. The World Bank loans money to developing countries for specific projects. The World Bank and the IMF programs are intended to benefit the world's poorest countries by freeing up resources for spending in the crucial areas of health, education, and rural development.

are engaged in some aspect of agricultural activities. Reliance on commodity exports, however, exposes the economy to the ups and downs of international price swings as well as to changes in weather. To end the country's dependence on fluctuating world prices for cocoa and coffee, the government encourages export diversification and intermediate processing of cacao beans. As a result, a light industrial sector has arisen, producing textiles, chemicals, and sugar for export. A few assembly plants for cars and other manufactured goods also have been built and are making significant headway.

Despite governmental gestures to expand the economy, agriculture, forestry, industry, manufacturing, and related activities hold on to their prime roles. They are the major export earners (some 70 percent of total exports) and the second-largest contributor to the country's gross domestic product (GDP), after the service sector.

AGRICULTURE

Côte d'Ivoire is the world's largest producer of cocoa and has a 40 percent share of the global market. More than a quarter of the population is engaged in the production of cocoa. The country is also the leading African producer

President Laurent Gbagbo greeted the $3 billion write-off by the IMF as good news, saying that the weight of the debt had become "a grave mortgage on the very future" of the country.

Rice fields. The government supports the cultivation of rice.

of coffee. These two commodities make up half of the country's export earnings. Besides cocoa and coffee, the government encourages the production of cotton, bananas, rubber, rice, and sugar. Along the coast, coconut trees and pineapples are also grown.

A variety of herbaceous plants are cultivated, including, yams, cassava, okra, sweet potatoes, peppers, rice, and plantain bananas. Cassava, more commonly known as tapioca, is widely grown because it does well in eroded soils.

Despite such massive domestic production, Côte d'Ivoire is among the top 10 importers of food in Africa. This disparity is because planted land is used primarily for commercial cash crops, and local people farm on a subsistence basis. Goats and sheep are the most significant livestock raised, since cows cannot be kept in areas infested with tsetse flies.

MANUFACTURING

The larger manufacturing industries include food-processing plants, lumber and textile mills, car assembly plants, steel container and aluminum sheet production, and oil refineries. Although the economy is still heavily dependent on agriculture, oil and gas production since 2006 have become more important engines of economic activity than cocoa. According to IMF statistics, earnings from oil and refined products were $1.6 billion in 2006. Côte d'Ivoire's offshore oil and gas production have resulted in substantial crude oil exports. In 2008 oil production reached 60,100 barrels per day. The hoped for 200,000 barrels per day by the end of the decade has not been met. Côte d'Ivoire has a complex refinery at Abidjan and a major pipeline project from the country's oil resources to Cameroon is being planned.

Côte d'Ivoire's offshore oil and gas production provide sufficient natural gas to fuel electricity exports to Ghana, Togo, Benin, Mali, and Burkina Faso.

The country's chemical industry centers around rubber production, as there are a number of rubber plantations that mainly export latex, the milky fluid that is the source of rubber. The government used to have a large stake in the three major companies involved in this industry, but it has sold its shares to private interests in the move to privatization.

FORESTRY

Côte d'Ivoire is a major exporter of hardwood. In the mid-1970s, timber overtook coffee to become the principal export. Since then, more sawmills and wood-processing plants have been built to produce plywood, crates, boxes, veneers, cabinets, and furniture. In recent years forest products accounted for $269 million in export value, coming in as Côte d'Ivoire's third most important source of foreign revenue behind cocoa and petroleum products. The major export markets for hardwood products are Italy, Spain, Germany, France, the Netherlands, the UK, India, Ireland, Senegal, and Morocco.

MINING

Although there are known reserves of copper, nickel, uranium, and manganese, mining is not a booming industry in Côte d'Ivoire. About 12,000 carats of diamonds used to be unearthed each year. In 2005, however, the United Nations banned the export of diamonds from Côte d'Ivoire. This ban was imposed as part of an arms embargo designed to prevent northern rebels from acquiring weapons illicitly through the sale of diamonds. Modern gold mining began in the early 1990s. Besides diamonds and gold, petroleum also is pumped into the economy from three offshore fields.

TOURISM

With a long coastal strip of beautiful beaches and lagoons, as well as protected wildlife and a lavish cultural heritage, Côte d'Ivoire has plenty to attract tourists. Tourism has the potential of becoming a leading industry,

A timber mill in San Pédro. Côte d'Ivoire is a major exporter of tropical woods and processed timber, used in home building and furnture making.

but a great many more capital resources need to be poured into the building of hotels and tourist inducements. The present government regards the further development of the tourist industry as a key priority.

TRADE

Foreign trading consists largely of imports of petroleum products, consumer goods, food, machinery, transportation equipment, and exports of coffee, cocoa, and timber. In 2007 annual exports totaled $8.5 billion, and imports amounted to $6.5 billion. Principal trading partners for exports are the Netherlands, France, Germany, and the United States. Chief partners for imports are France, Nigeria, Germany, Italy, and the United States. Principal imports from the United States are paper products, computer hardware and software, cosmetics, and toiletries.

Foreign direct investment also plays a key role in Côte d'Ivoire's economy, accounting for 40 to 45 percent of total capital in Ivorian firms. France is the most important investor by far, and in recent years French investment accounted for about one-quarter of the total capital in Ivorian enterprises.

CURRENCY

Côte d'Ivoire is a member of the eight-nation West African Monetary Union. The currency is the African Financial Community (CFA) franc with convertibility guaranteed by the French treasury. Since January 1, 1999, the West African CFA franc has been pegged to the euro at a rate of 655.957 CFA francs per euro. The West African CFA franc coins and banknotes are not accepted in countries using Central African CFA francs, and vice versa. In November 2009 one U.S. dollar equaled 441.420 West African CFA francs on average.

INFRASTRUCTURE

Côte d'Ivoire has a very good infrastructure by the standards of developing countries. There is a network of more than 8,000 miles (12,875 km) of paved roads, fine telecommunications services, including cellular phones, Internet access, and a public data communications network. This is a public network that allows the transmission of data from one location to another. The data transmitted is recorded in alphabetic, numeric, or pictorial form. It can even be a signal that represents a measurement. The construction and maintenance of roads has been privatized to improve efficiency and the condition of roads. Some dirt roads, which become impassable during the rainy season, have been replaced with paved roads.

There are two active ports. The port of Abidjan is the most modern in West Africa and the largest between Casablanca and Cape Town. A smaller port operates in San-Pédro. Abidjan has a fully equipped international airport, located at Port-Bouët. Up-to-date real estate developments exist for commercial, industrial, retail, and residential use.

Côte d'Ivoire has a reliable national network of paved roads.

Abidjan remains one of the most contemporary and livable cities in the region. Its school system is excellent by regional standards. It includes a number of excellent French language- and curriculum-based schools and an international school based on the U.S. curriculum.

The recent political and economic climate has set back Côte d'Ivoire's planned public investment program. Continued infrastructure development has been held up to question because of private sector doubt. A return to political and economic stability is important and necessary if Côte d'Ivoire is to realize its potential in the region.

MEETING GROWING ENERGY NEEDS

As more people migrate to the cities, energy needs increase dramatically. Although exploration teams first discovered natural gas in Côte d'Ivoire

Using renewable energy to speed up the drying of cacao beans to improve the quality of cocoa is catching on in Côte d'Ivoire. At cooperatives participating in the pilot project, solar-powered cacao bean dryers are installed in their greenhouses. Quickly reducing moisture in the beans to exportable levels and thereby increasing the likely amount of Grade A cocoa is the aim of this undertaking. There is concern in the industry that because so many private regulators are now licensed to evaluate quality, a poorer quality cocoa can get to the market. These private regulators place greater emphasis on volume to satisfy growing demands of cocoa, particularly during the peak harvesting period of October to February, resulting in farmers selling damp crop to them. Many cocoa growers are keen to go back to the traditional system where they alone evaluate the quality of their cacao beans.

in the 1980s, it was not until the mid-1990s that companies began to develop the valuable resource. It previously imported electricity from Ghana but now produces enough electricity for its own needs and is able to sell electricity to other African countries as well.

Before the discovery of natural gas, the annual production of electricity in the early 1990s totaled about 2 billion kilowatt-hours—much of it generated by hydroelectric installations. In 2006 Côte d'Ivoire generated 5.31 billion kilowatt-hours of electricity, consuming 2.9 billion kilowatt-hours itself and exporting the rest. Côte d'Ivoire's hydroelectric plants generate 37 percent of the country's electricity. Despite efforts to electrify rural areas, at least 700 villages in the nation are still without electricity. Demand for electricity in Côte d'Ivoire is expected to grow at a rate of about 10 percent per year.

WORKING CONDITIONS

The legal minimum working age in Côte d'Ivoire is 16, and the Ministry of Employment and Civil Service strictly enforces this provision in the civil service and in multinational companies. There are reports, nevertheless, of adolescents under 16 being employed in small workshops. A monthly minimum wage, last adjusted after the devaluation of the CFA franc in January 1994, is imposed by the government. Since then, the rate has not changed sharply, up or down. This rate is enforced for salaried workers employed by the government or registered with the social security office. A slightly higher minimum wage applies to construction workers. The minimum wage varies according to occupation, with the lowest set at $73.21 (36,607 CFA francs) per month. This meager earning is not enough to provide a decent standard of living for a family. Unfortunately, the majority of the labor force works in agriculture, forestry, or in the informal sector where minimum wage rules do not apply.

Unlike urban workers, farmers who sell their crops at the local markets usually do not have a steady income.

Through the Ministry of Employment and Civil Service, the government enforces a comprehensive labor code governing the terms and conditions of work for wage earners and salaried workers. Those employed in the formal, transparent sector are reasonably protected against unfair compensation, excessive hours, and arbitrary firing. The standard legal workweek is 40 hours. The law requires overtime payment on a graduated scale for additional hours. The code calls for at least one 24-hour rest period per week. Government labor inspectors can order employers to correct any substandard conditions, and a labor court can levy fines if an employer fails to comply. The code also provides for occupational safety and health standards. Nonetheless, in the sprawling informal sector of the economy the government's occupational health and safety regulations are enforced capriciously at best.

The labor code grants all citizens, except members of the police, gendarmerie, and military forces, the right to join unions, call strikes, and to bargain collectively. More than 100,000 workers belong to 231 unions grouped together in the government-sponsored General Workers Union.

ENVIRONMENT

A road cutting through one of Côte d'Ivoire's rain forests.

CHAPTER 5

ÔTE D'IVOIRE IS PARTICULARLY rich in flora and fauna. It has the highest level of biodiversity in West Africa with over 1,200 animal species and 4,700 plant species. Most of this diversity occurs in the country's rugged interior region. At one time Côte d'Ivoire was home to West Africa's largest rain forests. This prodigious biodiversity, however, is threatened by deforestation.

Since its independence in 1960, Côte d'Ivoire's forested area has fallen from 39.5 million acres to 24.7 million acres (16 million ha to 10 million ha), a fate that does not bode well for a country that is so highly dependent on the environment.

Côte d'Ivoire has a relatively diversified agricultural economy, thanks to the abundance of natural resources. About 66 percent of the population makes a living farming cocoa (cacao), coffee, palm oil, rubber, pineapples, bananas, and cotton. During the 1960s and '70s, timber exports were of major economic importance, ranking third behind cocoa and coffee as an export earner. Although output has fallen by more than 20 percent, Côte d'Ivoire remains the largest exporter of cocoa in the world. Overexploitation, meanwhile, has depleted many of the country's tropical timber resources.

Once the darling of West Africa, following its economic miracle in the 1980s, Côte d'Ivoire collapsed and weathered seven years of recession

Forest loss has made life more difficult for the people of Côte d'Ivoire who depend on the forests to meet their basic needs. With an economy so reliant on agricultural exports, the challenge facing Côte d'Ivoire is finding ways to continue feeding an ever growing population without permanently devastating the natural resources base on which all agricultural production hinges.

from 1987 to 1993. Resource depletion, declining productivity, and an inability to meet its foreign debt obligations were together blamed for Côte d'Ivoire's downfall. Political instability also hindered its ability to focus effectively on its environmental woes. Unfortunately, Côte d'Ivoire's environmental problems do not end with dwindling timber resources. Another looming peril is water pollution from industrial and agricultural effluents and from raw sewage.

A woman clearing the forest floor after cutting and burning the forest vegetation to make way for planting a crop.

FORESTS

Forests play a fundamental role in the basic functioning of the planet. They provide homes and habitats for multitudes of plant and animal species as well as for indigenous human communities. They also serve as a key defense against global warming and are indispensable partners in maintaining soil quality, limiting erosion, stabilizing hillsides, and modulating flooding. When forests are cleared, the soil's physical and chemical properties undergo far-reaching changes, leading to a loss of nutrients, accelerated soil erosion, and falling yields. Like most of West Africa, Côte d'Ivoire has suffered severe deforestation. As of 2005, less than 2 percent of the country's land was covered with primary forest.

Agriculture, uncontrolled fires, and logging for tropical hardwoods are the primary causes of forest loss. For most of the 20th century, loggers and farmers were turning trees into cash, a process that gave Côte d'Ivoire one of the highest living standards in Africa. According to the UN Food and Agriculture Organization (FAO), Côte d'Ivoire's forests are still disappearing, now at a rate of 2.9 percent a year, one of the highest deforestation rates on the planet.

The situation has only worsened in recent years. Prior to the outbreak of the civil war at the end of 1999, the Ivorian government devoted serious effort to make conservation a priority. It set aside 17 percent of the country in protected areas and took measures against illegal logging and poaching. The war, however, disabled law and order all across Côte d'Ivoire, allowing illegal loggers to plunder the country's dwindling forest reserves at breakneck rates.

CIVIL WAR AND ILLEGAL LOGGING

Trees can take 300 to 400 years to grow. Unfortunately, in times of war, long-term forest protection policies are abandoned for short-term financial gains. Such was the case in Côte d'Ivoire when a civil war flared up in September 2002. Giant old hardwood trees that were plentiful in the equatorial forests of southern and western Côte d'Ivoire were indiscriminately felled by a number of groups, from pro-government militia chiefs to rebel warlords and timber companies. Even ordinary villagers wanted a piece of the forest. In some cases there was no one to stop illegal loggers, while in others gangs wielded guns to force their way past forest guards and anyone else who may

Two botanists question loggers over suspected illegally cut logs from the Taï National Park.

Tanoé Swamps Forest in Côte d'Ivoire is one of the last remaining old growth forests in the country. It is home to many endangered plants and three highly endangered primates—the Miss Waldron's red colobus, the Geoffroy's black and white colobus, and the Diana roloway. It is believed that the last remaining population of the Miss Waldron's red colobus exists here. This rain forest has become threatened in recent days because a prominent consumer products company, Unilever, and other companies are poised to destroy it.

Unilever is one of the world's foremost food and personal care enterprises. Some of its consumer brands are Vaseline, Dove, and Lipton. Unilever publicly represents itself as a responsible palm oil company, being chair of the Roundtable for Sustainable Palm Oil. For example, it recently told Greenpeace that it will support a moratorium on rain forest and peat land destruction in Indonesia. Unilever had initially promised to buy only "sustainable" palm oil from lands not cleared of rain forests. In 2008, despite international protests, a palm oil company, PALM-CI, in which Unilever is a long-term investor, set about destroying the 14,826 acre (6,000 ha) Tanoé Swamps Forest in southeast Côte d'Ivoire to convert it to palm oil plantations. Drainage systems are currently being built on the periphery of the forest. Even with an international petition bearing some 8,000 signatures calling for the protection of the irreplaceable area, Unilever has done nothing to halt the destruction. The government of Côte d'Ivoire has also refused to protect the forest, repudiating appeals from many conservation NGOs.

If this forest is destroyed, the three primate species along with many plant species will without a doubt become globally extinct. Large amounts of carbon dioxide will be released from the carbon-rich swamp forest as well.

have tried to stop them. Corruption and poverty also had parts to play. The civil crisis resulted in increasing poverty, and many people in the countryside were so poor that they were willing to do anything for some cash.

Fortunes were certainly made from illegal logging in the freewheeling environment of war-torn Côte d'Ivoire. This has put the governance of the country's remaining natural resources under a lot of pressure.

Although the conflict is officially over, the country is still in a precarious situation under the interim government, and the future for forest conservation is unclear.

THE ACCRA DECLARATION

Côte d'Ivoire is a signatory to the Accra Declaration, which resulted from a Food and Agricultural Organization (FAO)/International Tropical Timber Organization (ITTO) workshop that was held in Accra, Ghana, in July 2008. The workshop explored the problems and possible solutions to the illegal extraction of forest resources in tropical West Africa. The countries in the region, including Côte d'Ivoire, are all interested in improving regional processes to integrate sustainability management of their forest resources.

Côte d'Ivoire recognizes that illegal extraction of forest resources, including timber, fuelwood, and wildlife, together with the associated trade of these products, seriously affects the stability of ecosystems. As a result of such intrusions, ecosystems become more vulnerable to climate change and degradation of soil and water resources. All these features of change contribute to an increase in rural poverty and endangerment of the quality of life of the whole population of the country.

Among the many recommendations put forth, Côte d'Ivoire agreed that governments in West Africa, along with participation from civil society and other stakeholder interests, should undertake a hard look at their forestry policies and laws and introduce new policies and laws as the need arises. The country also agreed that there is a need to introduce and implement wood tracking systems to promote transparency and effective monitoring systems throughout the forestry sector.

THE PROTECTED AREA PROJECT

On April 30, 2009, the World Bank approved the Protected Area Project, providing a grant of $2.54 million to help Côte d'Ivoire improve the sustainability management of the habitat and fauna of the Comoé National

Park. The great park, located in the northeastern region of Côte d'Ivoire, was initially added as a World Heritage Site because of the abounding diversity of plant life present around the Comoé River (also called the Komoé). There are also a large number of mammals in the park, including 11 monkey species. Ethnic groups around the park include the Lobi, located in Bouna and Téhini; the Koulabgo in Bouna and Nassian; the Dioula in Kong; and the Djimini in Dabakala. These clans are mostly dependent on agricultural and hunting activities. Because of improper management and continued poaching and overgrazing, the Comoé park was added to the list of World Heritage Sites in Danger in 2003.

The Protected Area Project aims to ensure that there are adequate institutional, financial, and technical capacities in place to properly manage the great park. It will also reach out to the diverse indigenous park communities—defined as the 200,000 people living on the fringes of the site—through its support of public awareness campaigns, biodiversity training, land management contracts, and alternate livelihoods.

POLLUTION CRISIS

One of the major environmental issues that Côte d'Ivoire faces is water pollution from sewage and industrial and agricultural effluents. Although this contamination has always been a problem in Côte d'Ivoire, a tragedy in 2006 brought the issue to the limelight, resulting in the resignation of a nine-month-old transitional government led by Charles Konan Banny, the deposed prime minister.

The dumping of 560 tons (508,023 kilograms) of toxic material in 14 open-air sites in Côte d'Ivoire's port city of Abidjan in 2006 led to the death of 17 people and widespread sickness. The toxic waste scandal focused a spotlight on the ways dangerous substances move around the globe, particularly between developed and developing countries.

This lethal waste was a mixture of oil residue and caustic soda used to rinse out the tanks of a Greek-owned cargo ship of a Dutch-based company, Trafigura. The company insisted that it had handed the waste over to an

"He who plants a tree before dying has not lived for nothing."
—Ivorian proverb

Ivorian firm, Tommy, to dispose of properly. Trafigura had planned to offload the waste in Amsterdam in July, but Dutch authorities said they had refused to accept it because it was too toxic. The Dutch firm stated that it had finally offloaded the waste in Abidjan on its way back from delivering a cargo of gasoline to Nigeria. Trafigura said it made this decision believing that the port "was one of the best equipped in West Africa" to treat it.

Litter choking the banks of a lagoon in Attecoube.

Investigations showed that the material was spread, allegedly by subcontractors, across the city and surrounding areas, dumped in waste grounds, public dumps, and along roads in populated areas. The sludge caused nausea, rashes, fainting, diarrhea, and headaches that affected tens of thousands of people. Almost 100,000 Ivorians sought medical attention for the effects of these dumped chemicals.

Three UN experts were dispatched to join six French waste disposal specialists in Côte d'Ivoire to help with an emergency plan to neutralize the toxic fumes emanating from the waste. A total of 36 health centers, 4 of them staffed by military personnel, were also on hand to attend to the victims of the poisoning.

Early in 2007 Trafigura paid $198 million for the cleanup to the Ivorian government without admitting wrongdoing. In return, the government pledged not to prosecute the company. Instead, an Ivorian court handed down separate jail terms to the two people it believed were to blame for the disaster. Nigerian national Salomon Ugborugbo, head of Tommy, was sentenced to 20 years in jail, whereas Essoin Kouao, who worked as a shipping agent at the Port of Abidjan, got only a 5-year jail term. A series of protests and resignations of Ivorian government officials followed this controversial outcome.

The tragedy of the Côte d'Ivoire pollution from dumped sludge in 2006 seemed almost inevitable because, for years, existing regulations on the dumping of waste had never been enforced.

IVORIANS

A young Ivorian mother carrying her baby boy
on her back.

CHAPTER 6

I N THE RURAL PARTS OF THE COUNTRY the Ivorian culture, in terms of food, religion, dress, ethnic roles, and daily life—its folkways—has remained unchanged for hundreds of years. Nonetheless, there has been a momentous shift in social identity. Ivorians now consider themselves citizens of Côte d'Ivoire first, then as members of their ethnic groups.

POPULATION CHARACTERISTICS

Côte d'Ivoire has about 20.6 million people, with an annual growth rate of 2.13 percent (2009 estimate), one of the highest in the world. Half the population is less than 16 years old. Besides the indigenous clans, who make up 77 percent of the population, there are the non-Africans, mostly French and Lebanese. These people constitute only about 3 percent of the population. The remaining 20 percent are Africans who are either immigrant workers or refugees who fled to Côte d'Ivoire as a result of civil wars in neighboring countries.

INDIGENOUS PEOPLES

Côte d'Ivoire is a diverse cultural puzzle with over 60 ethnic groups. The major groups came relatively recently from neighboring countries—

The population of Cote d'Ivoire is made up of many different groups of people. The majority are the indigenous people, who come from different ethnic groups, the largest of which is the Baule. Ivorians consider respect for one's family and elders to be very important. They are generally a warm and hospitable people.

the Malinke people came after the collapse of the Mali Empire in the 16th century; the Kru people migrated from Liberia around 1600; and the Senufo and Lobi tribes moved southward from Burkina Faso and Mali. It was not until the 18th and 19th centuries that the Akan people, the Baule, Agni, and Abron, migrated from Ghana into the eastern and central areas of the country. At around the same time, the Dioula moved from Guinea into the northwest. The vast ebb and flow of African clans has left a rich trail of language and custom.

A tribal chief with his subjects during a royal wedding.

Former Ivorian president Félix Houphouët-Boigny disliked the matrilineal aspect of Baule society. He thought it was a cause of family disunity.

BAULE is the largest ethnic group in Côte d'Ivoire, making up close to 20 percent of the country's population. They are a subgroup of the Akan peoples, who form 42.1 percent of the population. The Baule live in the central part of the country, primarily producing coffee and cocoa. They have a matrilineal social structure, although men occupy the important leadership positions and are expected to support any children of a deceased maternal relative, such as a sister. Baule villages are united into chiefdoms with the chief acting as protector, priest, judge, and ruler. It is a humanistic society—people, not material wealth, come first. A Baule would not say to a sibling, "Go to my room and get my jacket," but instead, "Go to the room and get the jacket." The possessive pronoun "my" does not exist. The Baule people are noted for their fine wooden sculpture, particularly for their ritual statuettes representing ghosts or spirits and for carved ceremonial masks.

THE AGNI AND ABRON migrated from the east and established powerful kingdoms on the fringes of the forest. Agni and Abron kings alike still receive allegiance from their people, adapting to modern institutions when necessary.

Every Friday at the king's palace, the sacred throne is shown to the people. Also on this day the king teaches history to young people and counsels his people. Family descent is through the maternal line, similar to the Baule, and polygamy for the male is the custom. Because they have retained their traditional monarchy, these people enjoy an elite status and political power in Côte d'Ivoire. The clans' main livelihood is subsistence farming with an emphasis on growing important cash crops such as cocoa and coffee. They mostly live in small villages and towns and are famous for their artwork with metal, wood, and clay.

THE SENUFO live in small villages of circular huts on the northern savanna. They settled in this place around 1600, and they speak at least four distinct languages. Although famous for their wood carving, masks, hand-painted Korhogo fabrics, pottery, dance, and music, the Senufo are predominantly an

The Senufo live in circular huts like this artfully decorated one.

agricultural people, cultivating rice, corn, yams, peanuts, and millet. The close relationship between the Senufo farmer and his land can be seen in their religious observances. Each village has a mythical ancestor in the form of an animal. This animal, or totem, is special to the Senufo and is a symbol of unity. The head of the family is the main authority figure who intercedes with the gods on behalf of his family to ensure good harvests. Aside from the lineage head, status distinctions are relatively few, although many people kept slaves from other societies well into the 20th century. The Senufo consider everyone in the village to be part of their extended family. Everyone in a village will eat and farm together. Each household contributes to the village storehouse, where the food is kept collectively.

A young Yacouba mother with her face covered with tree resin and red pepper, believed to relieve toothache.

Korhogo, the capital of the Senufo people, is some 311 miles (500 km) north of Abidjan and dates from the 13th century. The Senufo have two secret associations— the Poro cult for boys and the Sandogo cult for girls. Fellowships like these help to prepare the children for adulthood. The goal is to preserve the group's folklore, teach tribal customs, and instill self-control through rigorous physical and mental tests. The Poro boys' education lasts for seven years, ending with initiation rites involving circumcision, isolation, and instruction in the use of masks. Each community has a sacred forest spot where such training is done, and the uninitiated are not allowed to visit. They may watch the dance of the leopard men, however, a celebratory performance when the boys return from a training session in the forest. Ceremonies and dances mark the passage from one stage to the next. When a man reaches age 30, he is finally considered an elder who can offer adult advice to his people.

THE DAN, OR YACOUBA, tribe is one of the most interesting tribes in the country. The word *yacouba* in the local dialect means "all that begins by animated discussion." The Dan are noted for their dance masks, and dances are performed to mark all the important life events. So it is not surprising that some of the best dancers in the country come from this tribe. Besides masks, the Dan are also renowned for other crafts, including woven cloth, basketry, and wooden sculpture.

THE DIOULA live in the far northwest. They came from Guinea, bringing with them the Islamic faith. In addition to trading, their major activity, the Dioula are subsistence farmers of rice, millet (a grain), and peanuts. They also keep goats, sheep, poultry, and some cattle. This is a patrilineal society with the oldest male as head of his lineage. Villages tend to be grouped around men with the same clan name, and headmen are called imams, or religious leaders.

Men hunt and do the heavy farm work, while women tend to the children, cook, and perform other domestic and farm chores. Marriages are arranged, with a price paid to the bride's family, and some men have as many as three wives.

There are three social classes within the Dioula—the free born, originally considered the nobility but today consisting of farmers, merchants, and Islamic clerics; the artisan class of blacksmiths and leather workers; and the griots, entrusted with passing down oral tradition and the cultural heritage to succeeding generations. Oral literature is the treasury of Dioula history and values because so few Ivorians are literate.

A blend of Islam and traditional beliefs has resulted in healing and magic becoming very important. Holy men are called on for protective charms or the invocation of a curse on an enemy. Although many Dioula conceal their belief in magic, almost all carry a lucky charm.

THE LOBI live close to the Senufo in an isolated, relatively undeveloped part of the country. A proud people, they are known for their superb archery skills. Young boys are taught archery, their training divided into seven-year periods, so that by age 21 they all are able to hunt big game. Lobi women adorn themselves with inserted plates that stretch their lips.

Unlike many of the other ethnic groups, the Lobi have clung tightly to their traditions and seem uninterested in what is happening in the rest of the country.

THE KULANGO are closely related to the Lobi, their former enemies. The two tribes occupy the same region and share similar languages, customs, lifestyles, and religious beliefs. The Kulango are primarily farmers, growing crops such as yams, corn, peanuts, cotton, and watermelons. Some of them also breed goats, sheep, and cattle. The women gather wild fruits and nuts, whereas the men do most of the agricultural work.

Each Kulango village is made up of several small settlements of mud huts. The huts are clustered around a center court, which serves as a meeting place. Every settlement consists of several extended families, each of which is its

At one time the sustainability of the Poro cult was threatened by schools, which occupy a large part of a child's life. The schools taught a different system of thought and inquiry. The conflict, however, was resolved by the cult itself by combining the teachings of the schools with the laws, beliefs, and secrets of the Poro.

own economic unit. The male head of each extended family is responsible for offering sacrifices to the ancestral spirits. He is succeeded by his oldest sister's oldest son. The village chief and the religious headman handle all disputes and community affairs.

Most Kulango girls are betrothed while they are quite young. Marriages are arranged by either the girl's father or the extended family head. When a man marries, his bride may either join him or remain in her father's home. If she remains with her father, her daughters live with her and her sons join their father when they are able to walk and talk.

THE KRU have a long association with the sea. Fishing has long been their major activity, though now declining. Traditionally, the men loaded logging ships and made long sea passages with their cargoes. The Kru have tried to maintain their autonomy, but this has proved difficult, and they are becoming more assimilated into the Ivorian mainstream. Nevertheless, their traditional oral culture, accounting for numerous folk stories and morality tales, remains

Workers unloading tuna from a fishing boat in Abidjan. Fishing is no longer profitable for the Kru as their local port, Tabou, on the far western shore, has declined in importance compared with the ports at Abidjan and San Pédro.

The Lobi and the Kulango remain extremely steadfast in their religions and folkways. When Islam was introduced to the country, they resisted it. They have rejected many aspects of European acculturation and lack the overall preoccupation with economic progress that characterizes much of the nation.

Côte d'Ivoire cooperates with the United Nations High Commissioner for Refugees (UNHCR) in health, education, and food distribution programs for refugees. Following the outbreak of the Liberian civil war, which killed 10 percent of its 2.5 million people and displaced 700,000 others, many sought refuge in Côte d'Ivoire. At one point there were more than 300,000 Liberian refugees in Côte d'Ivoire. Today, little more than 30,000 Liberians remain in the country. When the civil war broke out in Côte d'Ivoire in 2002, these exiles were in imminent danger because anti-Liberian sentiments had hit an all-time high. President Gbagbo blamed the failed 2002 coup on mercenaries from English-speaking nations, putting Liberian refugees in danger, because Liberia, unlike Côte d'Ivoire, is an Anglophone country. These refugees were targeted by the military and armed youths who accused them of being associated with antigovernment forces. Thousands of Liberians were made homeless as security forces set their houses on fire. The UNHCR, fearing that these beleaguered refugees would be massacred, assisted more than 2,500 of them to voluntarily repatriate back to Liberia.

strong. Kru families are patrilineal, and marriage is polygamous. Not known to have kept slaves themselves, they exported slaves from neighboring tribes during the height of the slave trade.

MINORITIES

Non-Ivorian Africans who reside in Côte d'Ivoire make up almost one-fifth of the total population. Their numbers are growing as quickly as the crime rate, thus many Ivorians attribute the high crime rate to these foreigners. As a result, foreign Africans are often subject to discrimination, sometimes even harassment.

There are also a number of other foreigners living in Côte d'Ivoire, including some 130,000 Lebanese and 14,000 French—around 3 percent. Many Protestant missionaries from the United States and Canada also reside in the nation. In November 2004 some 10,000 French and other foreign nationals were evacuated from Côte d'Ivoire because of attacks from pro-government youth militias. Many of these abused evacuees are trickling back, however.

IVORIAN CHARACTER

Respect for one's family, elderly people, and women is a distinctive quality of Ivorians. Ivorians are very hospitable people—they are always ready to welcome strangers into their homes for some food and drink. They are also extremely polite and really enjoy inquiring about a visitor's health and family. Ivorians are a gentle and relaxed people. To the Ivorian, trust is very important in a relationship, whether one of business or friendship. Without trust, nothing much gets done.

SOCIAL CUSTOMS

In the traditional Ivorian greeting it is important to inquire about a person's health, family, work, or the weather. Getting down to the business at hand immediately in any encounter is considered rude. Women do not shake hands with each other but instead kiss each other three times on the cheeks, starting with the left cheek and alternating sides. Men, however, typically shake hands. At social functions, it is appropriate for men to shake hands with everyone when entering and again when leaving. Eye contact is usually avoided, particularly between father and child. It is considered extremely rude to stare at other people. Giving gifts is important, especially to those who are higher in the social hierarchy or are respected people. For example, if a mother-in-law comes for a visit, she would expect a gift. The thinking behind giving presents is that if God has been good to you, then you should be happy to spread that good fortune around.

DRESS

Ivorians place great importance on clothing. Their clothing can be divided into two types—traditional and casual attire. Traditional formal dress for men is pants and shirt beneath a long embroidered robe that reaches to the ground. Their more casual clothes resemble Western-style pajamas. For women, traditional dress is also a long embroidered robe. For daily wear, a woman may put on a loose blouse and wrap a piece of colorful cloth around her waist for a skirt. Ivorian women also like to tuck their hair neatly under beautiful coiled cloths with bright flower motifs. This is a practical and fashionable method to keep their hair out of the way while they work. Decorative fabrics are handmade in small cottage industries.

Women wearing colorful traditional headdresses in Grand Bassam.

SOCIAL HIERARCHIES

From the 1960s to '80s there was a wide gap between the ruling elite and those who were ruled. The wealthy, urban, and educated privileged minority received most of the benefits and had access to the country's resources. Political appointments were typically accompanied by land concessions in Abidjan. This resulted in a scarcity of building lots and high rents for everyone else. Cabinet ministers got monthly housing allowances and lived in relative luxury. Personal wealth and government service became closely linked. For ordinary people who lived in rural areas, secondary education and access to health care were nonexistent. Employment was a very significant indicator of social status. Government employees earned far more than the national average, whereas many people were unemployed in the countryside. In general, the difference in the daily lives of the urban elite and the poor majority was enormous.

Since the 1990s there have been some changes in this state of affairs. The middle class is expanding as the living standards of low-wage workers rise. Opportunities for social mobility are slowly increasing. Regrettably, the living conditions of the very poor have changed little, and they remain alienated from the overall economic progress of the country. Troublesome serious inequalities in the distribution of wealth persist.

LIFESTYLE

Ivorians often balance containers and other objects on their heads while walking.

CHAPTER 7

UNLIKE MOST OF AFRICA WHERE rural life is predominant, in Côte d'Ivoire about half the population lives in cities. More and more country peasants are forced to find a living elsewhere as deforestation makes the land too barren to grow crops.

Increasingly, young people, mostly men, are drawn to the cities where they believe they will find a better standard of living. So they quit the countryside and head to the bustling urban centers. The most popular destinations are Abidjan and Bouaké.

Unfortunately, these young people fail to realize that the transition from village life to a diverse, metropolitan environment can be extremely difficult, particularly after the conflict in 2002.

Poverty has increased from 38.2 percent in 2002 to 49 percent in 2008. In addition, there is massive population displacement and rising unemployment. But one thing is certain, whether Ivorians are living in the countryside or in the cities, the traditions of hospitality, family, and kinship are loyally sustained.

ROLE OF THE FAMILY

In Côte d'Ivoire the extended family is the basic social unit. The family is linked to a larger society through clans, called lineages, traced through male or female descent. An entire village is frequently made up of one single clan. Members of the same clan generally do not find

Except for those living in the cities, almost all Ivorians dwell in compounds that are groups of strongly built mud huts clustered around central courtyards. In major cities people live in apartments or houses. About 49 percent of Côte d'Ivoire's population lives in a city, as many are convinced that more job opportunities can be found there.

a marriage partner within the group. Lineage ties enable people to live in harmony and foster a community spirit. Older members teach the young the history of their clan and enable them to cultivate a sense of social responsibility.

Every child born is a child of the entire village, and the child's success or failure is felt by everyone in the village. The responsibility to raise children and teach them social values belongs to everyone. This connection to others is of paramount importance. It is instilled at an early age, so that even if people leave the village, they will always act in the knowledge that they are a representative of their family and village. Thus they should never bring disgrace on those still at home. This reinforces the vital concept of community above self.

ROLE OF WOMEN

Traditionally, a woman's role is to be a wife and mother. Boys are taught from an early age to always respect girls because one day the girls will be wives and mothers. Taking care of the family budget and children, particularly the girls, is the woman's responsibility. In Ivorian society

Women together pounding millet in a Senoufo village.

the relationship between a mother and her daughter is a very special one because they spend a great deal of time together.

A woman is also expected to perform most of the less physical farming tasks, such as growing the vegetables and feeding the animals. For the fortunate women who can afford to attend school and complete their education, there are rosier opportunities. An increasing number of women are employed in important sectors of the economy, such as medicine, business, and university teaching. Politically, women also have more say in the implementation of social policies. At the highest political level, Simone Gbagbo, the wife of the current president, holds a powerful position as head of the ruling party's parliamentary bloc. Few women complete their education, however. According to 2008 statistics, illiteracy affects 63.2 percent of all women and 73.6 percent of poor women.

The older, traditional woman may find it difficult to comprehend the choices that some modern Ivorian women have to make today, compared with the choices she had when she was their age. Some modern women no longer accept their subordinate role in society, asserting that such traditional practices as female circumcision and early marriage are harmful to their health. Thus they openly challenge many tribal conventions and folk beliefs.

CHILDREN

Educational services expanded considerably after independence. Primary education is free of charge and officially mandatory for six years, although this rule is not strictly enforced. Many children leave school at an early age, particularly girls and those living in rural areas. Children have to work on the farm as soon as they are old enough to do chores. For many, helping out the family takes priority over school. By working beside their parents, children learn from an early age the values of their family and village. Girls are taught by their mothers, and boys mostly talk with their fathers and other males. When the girls get married and leave home, the responsibility of taking care of the old folks at home falls on the sons. Rather than telling children what to do or not to do, Ivorian parents

Many Ivorian children do not get the opportunity to finish school.

get their message across by reciting simple stories with morals that have been handed down from generation to generation—delightful fables with a punch.

IVORIAN MEN

An Ivorian man is brought up, first and foremost, to provide for his wife and family. An ability to do this well results in higher social status for the individual. The continuing custom of polygamy depends on earning ability, because only a man who is doing well can afford to have more than one wife. A man will look for another wife only if he can provide for her. The chosen woman and her family ensure that this is the case before agreeing to the marriage.

The last 20 years has seen many young men leaving their villages to seek better lives in the cities, where there are more job opportunities and they can earn more money. This migration has brought about many social problems. Most young men find life in the cities to be very different from life at home. In a village, for instance, it is perfectly natural to eat with any family and stay in any hut, but in the cities one must pay for food and lodging. If the young man is poor, he will have to depend on relatives who live there.

Ivorian washermen doing laundry in a river near Abidjan.

LIFE-CYCLE EVENTS

Ceremonies, whether happy or sad, are an integral part of Ivorian society. Special events, such as births, weddings, and funerals, are given great attention. A birth is usually celebrated for one to two days. If the family is Christian, the child is baptized. Guests give the parents a gift, which is usually a small amount of money, and after the church ceremony, everyone gathers for a feast.

Marriage is an important social institution, providing continuity and cohesion in society, and it is always an occasion for great joy and celebration. The marriage ceremony, attended only by relatives and the closest friends of the couple, is usually held at the mayor's office. The ceremony is the culmination of a week of activities, including visits to relatives, feasts, and exchanges of gifts.

For the exchange of vows, the bride decorates herself from head to toe. Guests bring wedding gifts of gold, silver, animals, food, and basic supplies for the couple to set up housekeeping together. The wedding guests are all invited to a big feast with music and dancing.

STANDARD OF LIVING

About half the Ivorian population is urban, and many people live in crowded slums in Abidjan and Bouaké. This is a result of the high population growth rate and a simultaneous economic decline since the 1980s. Urban centers attract large numbers of rural migrants who come either as permanent settlers or as short-term workers. There are considerably more amenities in the cities of Abidjan and Bouaké, where many rich people live, than in smaller towns. The standard of living in Côte d'Ivoire's cities is higher than in most African countries.

But daily life for the average young man looking for work and trying to survive can be tough. Government efforts to implement major structural reforms have led to disastrous results for many. The unemployment rate is sky-high in the cities as is also the poverty rate. Although Côte d'Ivoire is making some small progress in lifting its overall standard of living, its health services, and literacy, it is moving at a snail's pace.

URBAN LIVING

When a nuclear family living in the city is joined by their cousins and nephews from the countryside, their small rented apartment becomes very cramped. The head of the household usually pays all the bills if he has a job and allows

Few residents of the slums have access to electricity, a clean water supply, or a sewage system. Children defecate in streams filled with garbage, and women are forced to do their washing in the same foul streams.

his cousins and nephews, or any relative in need, to stay for free at his house. Ivorians have long embraced their duty to care for their extended family. When relatives approach them for help, they cannot turn them away because to do so would risk scorn and isolation.

Those who have no relatives in the cities usually live in crowded slum quarters. Shantytowns have mushroomed around Abidjan in recent years. About 15 percent of the capital's population lives in these packed slums.

RURAL LIVING

Rural living features in Côte d'Ivoire vary among locations and the clans. Generally, each village consists of several small settlements. The settlements include a number of mud huts with cone-shaped roofs made of palm leaves, although corrugated metal is now more frequently used. Dwellings are clustered around a central open area that is often used as a gathering place. Every settlement is made up of several extended families, each of which is its own economic unit. The Senufo live in villages of circular huts with unusual, elaborately carved wooden doors.

A typical day for a rural family begins early. Rising at about 4 A.M., the men are the first to go to their land and start working. The women must first clean their hut, get fires burning, and look after the children. Then they join their husbands later in the morning, taking care of the vegetable crops, such as peppers, potatoes, and peanuts. The men are responsible for clearing land of trees and brush so that yams, bananas, or other crops can be planted.

Farming is hard work. The farmers have to spend long hours under the scorching sun. The women return home around midafternoon to tend to their children and to cook the family's dinner. For the men, the day ends when the sun sets.

EDUCATION AND LITERACY

Education in Côte d'Ivoire is free through university level, and elementary school, which lasts for six years, is compulsory. After four years of secondary education, students take exams. If they perform well, they get a certificate. After that, another three years is spent studying for the secondary school certificate required to enter a university. Universities in Côte d'Ivoire include the National University of Côte d'Ivoire, the University of Abobo-Adjamé, and the University of Cocody, all three of which are in Abidjan, and the University of Bouaké. There are also several colleges in the country, primarily centered around Abidjan and Yamoussoukro. A large number of Ivorian students study abroad.

Elementary school students in Bouaké. Political instability has disrupted education for many young Ivorians.

During the 1970s the educational system in Côte d'Ivoire was the envy of other African countries. The government had heavily subsidized education and even experimented with televised lessons, one of the few African nations to do so. The recession in the 1980s, however, led to cutbacks in funding. Political instability has also resulted in the halting of educational system development as many schools were closed in areas occupied by rebel forces. The quality of teaching has dropped sharply, especially at the primary level, owing to the lack of qualified teachers.

The national primary school enrollment rate fell from 79.5 percent in 2001 to 2002 to 54.4 percent in 2004 to 2005. The enrollment rate in secondary education is estimated to be at a disheartening 30 percent.

The literacy rate of Côte d'Ivoire is 48.7 percent. This is slightly lower than the regional average, though it is significantly lower than the world average. Although elementary education is compulsory, this requirement is not effectively enforced. A great many children leave school after only a few years. Large numbers of parents prefer to send only their boys for an education, a trend noticeable throughout the country but that is more pronounced in rural areas. The government is aware that its national literacy rate is not acceptable. A system in which a quarter of children, particularly

Fortunately, in a country with such a low literacy rate, there lives a man who understands the important role of education to future development in a world where trained skilled workers are required. He is Ambassador Pierre Kipré of Côte d'Ivoire. Formerly, he was a minister of national education of Côte d'Ivoire. He has plans to provide more education in rural areas, as well as correspondence schools and apprenticeship programs. One lingering difficulty, however, is that teachers are paid very little, and many teaching vacancies exist because the expanding private sector offers far greater pay.

As education minister, he drew up three literacy programs that gave priority to women and children. These programs were unveiled during the 1998 celebration of International Literacy Day in Abidjan and were called "One Literate Woman, Three Children Educated." The first part of the five-year program was expected to help 25,000 women learn to read and write and to get 75,000 rural children into school. The second phase focus was on girls, who at present are the most grievously deprived of education. The third phase aimed to educate 10,000 women every year. Minister Kipré stated that the goal was to increase the national literacy rate to 85 percent by the year 2010. It was hoped that by that date some 70 percent of Ivorian women would be able to read and write. Unfortunately, that goal has not been met.

girls and rural youngsters, do not go to school at all is lamentable. This characterization is slowly changing as the political situation stabilizes. In 2006 the government was able to hold examinations throughout the whole country, and recent school years went off smoothly.

HEALTH SERVICES AND CHALLENGES

Health services in Côte d'Ivoire were comparatively good before the late 1980s. The economic crisis, however, made it extremely hard for the government and burdened medics to meet the needs of a rapidly growing population. In the 1990s the ratio of Ivorians to doctors was 17,847 to 1. In 2002 the civil war severely disrupted health-care services in the northern part of the country.

Some health facilities were destroyed, and many medical personnel fled the region. Those who remained were concentrated in urban areas for the sake of their security. Thankfully, many such medical personnel have since returned to their deserted health stations.

Western-style hospitals are located in Abidjan, Bouaké, Daloa, and Korhogo, and struggling clinics can be found in other areas. There are also many practitioners of indigenous forms of medicine.

Chronic malnutrition, resulting in stunted growth and other afflictions, is one of the most serious health problems for young children in the country. Children in rural areas are twice as likely to be underweight than those in the cities. Another grave problem is river blindness, a disease transmitted by black flies. More than half of poor households do not have access to clean drinking water and are exposed to waterborne diseases, but this peril is much higher in the northern rural savanna and the eastern rural forest.

Since the late 1990s, HIV/AIDS has been a rapidly expanding problem. HIV/AIDS infections and other sexually transmitted diseases are spreading quickly. At least 7 percent of the population is living with HIV/AIDS, ranking Côte d'Ivoire the 17th nation in the world with the greatest number of HIV/AIDS cases. In 2007 around 38,000 people in Côte d'Ivoire died from AIDS alone.

To tackle these problems, the government earlier initiated a health-development plan for a 10-year period, 1995 to 2005. The plan aimed to improve the population's access to health services. Sadly, though, it was unable to bring the plan to completion because of the war-torn division of the country and a stoppage of funding for numerous health projects.

A health worker administering yellow fever vaccine in Koumassi.

The health situation in Côte d'Ivoire is poor, and HIV/AIDS infection and sexually transmitted diseases (STDs) are spreading rampantly across the country.

RELIGION

An Ivorian boy praying in the Grand Mosque at Agboville, north of Abidjan.

THERE ARE THREE MAJOR RELIGIONS in Côte d'Ivoire. An estimated 38.6 percent of the people are Muslims who practice Islam, whereas approximately 32.8 percent are Christians—mostly Roman Catholics or from various Protestant churches. About 25 percent of the population practices traditional religions.

The nation's constitution provides for freedom of religion, and the government generally respects this right. Some ethnic discrimination—

Ivorian Muslims praying in a street in Abobo district.

Many different belief systems are observed in Côte d'Ivoire. Traditional religions continue to predominate among rural communities. The percentage of the population that practices Christianity has increased in recent years. Present also are followers of the Harrist faith, a religion indigenous to Côte d'Ivoire.

paralleling differences in religious affiliation and resulting from the ongoing political conflict—continues.

Although the country's political conflict lay along ethnic rather than religious lines, political and religious affiliations tended to follow ethnic lines; hence some religious groups have been especially hard hit by the conflict. For instance, many ethnic northerners are Muslims, and as a result, many Muslims were assumed to be rebels and rebel sympathizers by the government during the civil war and were targeted as suspects.

Fortunately, strong efforts by religious and civil society groups have helped prevent the political crisis from turning into a religious conflict, but there still survives some societal discrimination against Muslims and followers of traditional indigenous religions.

ISLAM

Muslims make up about 38.6 percent of the population. Islam was founded by the Prophet Muhammad. Born in A.D. 570, an Arab, he left Mecca in 610 and traveled while preaching his divine revelations.

The imposing Yamoussoukro Mosque.

Theoretically no religion is dominant and no faith is officially favored in Côte d'Ivoire. The government permits open religious practices and does not restrict religious teaching.

After Muhammad's death in 632, his followers collected his revelations, putting them into a book called the Koran. This became the holy scripture of Islam. Another book was also compiled—the Hadith, which is a collection of Muhammad's sayings. These beloved observations were memorized and preserved by his companions. Muslims view the Hadith as an additional source of spiritual guidance, besides the Koran. There are several denominations or creeds within Islam, though most Ivorians are Sunni. Sufism is also widespread, and there are some Shia.

There are five primary religious obligations that each Muslim must fulfill in his or her lifetime. They are called the Five Pillars of Islam.

1. SHAHADAH (sha-HAHD-ah) is the profession of faith. Muslims bear witness to the oneness of God by reciting the creed, "There is no deity but Allah" and "Muhammad is His servant and messenger." This simple, yet profound statement, expresses a Muslim's complete acceptance of, and total commitment to, the message of Islam.

2. SALAT (sa-LAHT) is prayer. Muslims pray five times a day—at dawn, noon, midafternoon, sunset, and nightfall. Prayers link the worshiper to Allah. There are a number of rituals and movements to be performed while praying, so that a prayer takes some time to perform. There are no priests in Islam. Instead, a learned man chosen by his peers leads the prayers in a mosque.

3. ZAKAT (za-KAHT) means almsgiving, or giving up of one's surplus wealth. When Muslims give alms to the poor and needy, they must do it with sincerity and compassion and not expect something in return.

4. SAWM (sa-AHM) is fasting. During the holy month of Ramadan, Muslims go without food and drink during daylight hours as an act of worship. Ramadan is the time when Muslims seek a richer perception of God. Fasting teaches them patience, unselfishness, moderation, willpower, discipline, a spirit of social belonging, unity, and brotherhood.

Peace is the dominant theme in Islam. Peace with Allah, with one's soul, with the family and friends, and with all living creatures. To disturb the peace of anyone or any creature in any shape or form is strictly prohibited.

5. HAJJ (HAHJ) means pilgrimage. It is the duty of every Muslim who is fit and can afford it to make at least one pilgrimage to Mecca. For some this involves a lifetime of savings. It is not unusual for families to save for years and then send only one member to represent the entire family.

MOSQUES

Muslims worship Allah in a mosque. The early mosques looked like the courtyard of Muhammad's house, the place where the first Muslims gathered to listen to his sermons. Most mosques today are closed to non-Muslims because of an increased emphasis on the sanctity of mosques. Muslims of all creeds are in theory free to worship in any mosque, but in reality, a traveling Muslim will try to find a mosque that is used by others of his own creed.

A mud mosque in Ferkéssédougou. Wooden stakes help to support the earthen walls.

The design of mosques evolved from very simple to complex structures in a short time. The addition of minarets, or towers from which the calls to prayer are made, was inspired by other religious buildings. The idea of adorning mosques was copied from churches, and some mosques are very beautiful, with decorative calligraphy and depictions of flowers and geometric shapes. Over time, Muslims started to add rooms to mosques to use for travelers, the ill, classes for boys learning the Koran, a library, or a special room for praying women. Devout Muslims often live in mosques. A fountain or other facility is present so worshipers can wash their hands for purification before prayer. When entering a mosque, a visitor must take off his shoes. Entering a mosque has to be done with the right foot first, while reciting blessings to

Muhammad and his family. A person inside a mosque will talk softly so that he does not disturb worshipers who are praying.

Women in Côte d'Ivoire are not prevented by the Islamic faith from entering mosques, but actually, for a long time they have not been welcomed. Mosques can be closed to women, either by local rules or by long-standing usage.

Although it is considered more meritorious to pray in a mosque with other people, a Muslim may pray almost anywhere—in the fields, offices, factories, or universities. The Friday prayer or sermon at a mosque is considered to be compulsory for all male Muslims.

CHRISTIANITY

Christianity, Africa's second most widespread religion, was introduced to northern Africa in the first century A.D. By the fourth century A.D., the faith had migrated to other parts of Africa. Christianity has survived in some African countries, but in many others it has been supplanted by Islam. Today, Christian subgroups found in the country include the Roman Catholic Church, the Jehovah's Witnesses, the Seventh-day Adventist Church, the Southern Baptist Church, the Coptic Christians, and the Church of Jesus Christ of Latter-day Saints, or Mormons. The largest Protestant denomination is the Protestant Methodist Church of Côte d'Ivoire.

Roman Catholicism in Côte d'Ivoire was reintroduced by French missionaries during the colonial period, particularly among the Agni people. It is still most prevalent among them. In general, Roman Catholicism is practiced by the middle class and urban south. Villages adopt certain patron saints and honor them on secular and religious holidays. The first African Roman Catholic mission was established in 1895, but the first African priest was not ordained until 1934. In the 1980s the church started seminaries and schools throughout the country, and a large cathedral, Saint Paul's, was built in Abidjan. In 1990 the former president, Félix Houphouët-Boigny, funded the building of the Basilica of Our Lady of Peace, in the style of the Basilica of Saint Peter, in Rome.

This religion is the largest and oldest Protestant denomination in the country. Founded in 1914 by a Liberian, William Harris, Harrism is considered more an African religion than a Western one taught by white missionaries. Traveling through Ghana and Côte d'Ivoire, Harris led a simple life. He attracted followers by preaching against adultery, theft, and lying, and condemning excessive wealth. Harris regarded as ignorant the traditional belief in the power of charms against evil. His style of Christianity was open to all people, and he succeeded partly because he was African and partly because he showed no gender discrimination. Thus women, as well as men, converted to Harrism. Earlier Christian missionaries had not understood the importance of matrilineal descent in Ivorian society.

Although the teachings and beliefs of Harrism were not really in opposition to the colonial authorities, in 1915 a nervous French governor asked Harris to leave. This revitalized his church tremendously, and many small Harrist churches sprang up along the coast. By 1925 Methodist missionaries were continuing his work among the lagoon people of the southwest, and Harrism became recognized as a branch of Methodism.

PLACES OF WORSHIP

BASILICA OF OUR LADY OF PEACE The basilica, situated in Félix Houphouët-Boigny's birthplace, Yamoussoukro, sits on a massive 7.4-acre (3-ha) plaza with a marble Roman-style entrance. It cost $400 million to build, and the maintenance costs are an annual $1.5 million. With a towering cross on top, it claims to be the tallest church in the world. In September 1990 Pope John Paul II visited Côte d'Ivoire for the third time and consecrated the basilica. Since then it has been visited by more than two million people and is becoming a pilgrimage stop for many Catholics around the world.

The floor space of Our Lady of Peace is enormous—it can hold 300,000 people. The cathedral has 36 beautiful stained-glass windows, the glass all handblown in France. All the figures depicted in the windows are Caucasian except for one solitary black pilgrim, who resembles Houphouët-Boigny. He is portrayed kneeling at the feet of Christ.

About 120,000 Ivorians were personally baptized by William Harris, the founder of Harrism.

SAINT PAUL'S CATHEDRAL is an attractive modern cathedral with a big tower that affords a panoramic view of the city of Abidjan. It was designed by an Italian architect, Aldo Spiritom, and consecrated by Pope John Paul II in 1985.

TRADITIONAL RELIGIONS

Many Ivorians continue to follow traditional religions involving ancestor worship. Each ethnic group has its own distinctive religious practices, but some elements are common to all. All traditional religions are animistic, which means that people believe everything has a soul. They also accept the notions of a supreme being and reincarnation. Besides the creator, there are numerous lesser gods that Ivorians pray to for good health, bountiful harvests, and the blessing of many children, and whom they honor in village celebrations. They worship ancestral spirits also, believing in their protective oversight.

The building of Saint Paul's Cathedral points to a shift toward modern architecture styles.

Ancestral spirits are those members of the family or lineage who have died and transformed into spirits. They remain in constant contact with the living. Through various rituals, the living kin seek their blessings and protection. The principal role of the ancestral spirits is to protect the tribe. The spirits are the real owners of the land—the villagers cannot sell it or they would incur the wrath of their forebears. Magic is also commonly practiced in traditional rites. Good magic keeps the evil spirits safely away. Medicine men dispense charms, tell fortunes, and give advice on how to avoid danger. They also bless grisgris, which are charmed necklaces that ward off specific evils. If the grisgris has not been blessed by the medicine man, it won't work.

A roadside memorial built to honor a deceased Ivorian.

The Senufo religious leaders, or marabous, officiate at ceremonies, honor the gods, and advise people on how to cope with their problems. Sometimes they act as doctors, because many illnesses are thought to have spiritual causes.

The Agni and Baule have a single supreme god or creator figure, Nyame, and a number of subordinate gods who inhabit trees, water, and animals. Below them are still lesser deities whose power is invoked through protective charms. The ancestral spirits who affect the people's daily lives are always in contact with the living and can directly influence a person's fortunes in his present life. Thus it is important for the living to seek their blessings and protection through various rituals. Ancestral spirits are always consulted, sometimes even offered food and drink. Failure to perform such rites makes the spirits angry and can result in misfortune.

The Kru believe in a second god besides the creator. This god is a devil who works against the creator resulting in humans having a balance of good and evil within themselves. The crux is to maintain this balance of the antagonistic features in their daily lives.

The Dioula believe that their god created the world and four sets of twins. These eight twins were commanded to populate earth and to teach their children to grow crops.

The Lobi think of divination as a means of determining death, disease, or any misfortune. Diviners act like counselors, not predicting the future but suggesting some action to help people cope with their problems.

The Kulango believe in a god who is not worshiped but is addressed in his association with "mother earth." This earth god is the god of the whole tribe. During disasters or hard times, the Kulango pray to the spirits of their ancestors and make offerings to them of mashed yams.

A BLEND OF THE THREE RELIGIONS

Over the centuries, both Christian and Islamic rites and beliefs have been incorporated into indigenous religions. New religious movements that contain elements from the different religions have also been formed. Led by individual prophets, these separatist groups mix beliefs from different sources to help people deal with the demands of daily life. Most popular among minority groups resisting domination by stronger groups, such religions are evolving and finding a place among Ivorians. For example, although many of the Agni have remained Roman Catholic, their neighbors, the Baule, have followed the prophets who promise good fortune to those who adhere to the new dogmas.

A Muslim imam in the town of Niofouin, famous for its blend of animist and Muslim religions.

LANGUAGE

A spread of Ivorian newspapers featuring headlines about President Barack Obama's inauguration.

T HE OFFICIAL NATIONAL LANGUAGE of Côte d'Ivoire is French, a legacy of the earlier colonial administration.

The name of the country is French, meaning Ivory Coast. Educated Ivorians are bilingual, speaking French and their mother tongue, which is the language of their village and ethnic group. With 60 different ethnic groups, this means that there are as many languages spoken in the country.

SPOKEN LANGUAGES

The 60 languages of Côte d'Ivoire are all grouped under the Niger-Congo language family, a group of languages widely spoken in western, northern, and southern Africa. Languages of this family are called tone

An Ivorian woman reading a newspaper in French.

Students learning French, a compulsory subject in high school.

languages because tones serve phonetically to distinguish the meanings of words. Totally different meanings are distinguished merely by changes in the pitch of a single syllable. These different pitches are crucial to understanding exactly what is said. In such cases, a single word may have a number of different meanings, depending on which syllable is intoned higher or longer or given more stress.

There are four branches of the Niger-Congo family in Côte d'Ivoire—the Kwa, the Mande, the Kru, and the Gur groups. The Kwa branch consists of the Baule language, which is spoken by over two million people. The Abron and Agni languages also belong to this group. The Mande branch includes the Dioula language, spoken by over a million people. The Dan language, also belonging to the Mande branch, has existed for 5,000 years! It is considered the oldest offshoot of the family. The Kru branch consists of the Kru language. The Gur branch refers to the Senufo language, which is spoken by over one million people. The Lobi and Kulango languages are among the languages that belong to the Gur branch. Each of these languages also

Some African languages are spoken by relatively few people. The Ega language, for example, is spoken by only 2,500 people.

Traditional griots are either attached to leading households in African societies or serve as freelance poets. In either role, they exercise their vast knowledge of history, language, and the lineage of their patrons by praise singing, commentary, and instrumental accompaniment. Yet none of these descriptions quite illustrates their unique status in Dioula society. They are educated and wise, and they use their detailed knowledge of history to shed light on present-day dilemmas. In the past, griots tutored princes and gave council to kings. Now, a rich Dioula family employs its own griot to advise them and help them negotiate matters with other families. Griots also arrange marriages and mediate disputes, relying on their profound understanding of each family's history.

has many dialects. Thus people living in different regions have different pronunciations of the same words. For a characteristic example, the Dioula language has 22 dialects.

FRENCH

French belongs to the Indo-European language family. It is taught in the schools, so anyone who can afford to attend school will be able to speak and write French. Although the language was imposed on Ivorians during colonial days and is not a native language, it provides people with a lingua franca—a common communication tool. Without French, problems would arise when people try to converse in 60 different languages. It would be impossible to choose any local language as the official one because not more than a 10th of the population can understand any single native language.

ORAL TRADITIONS

Ivorian cultural expression remains very distinct today, particularly in its oral forms. Although writing traditions exist, Ivorians are primarily a vocal people, as are most Africans. Throughout their history, Ivorians have regarded oral language as a mighty force. All the people share and value this heritage. In a country where many ethnic languages coexist and a colonial language was imposed on everyone, it requires incredible effort to preserve a written literature for each ethnic tongue. Moreover, widespread illiteracy undermined any such concepts. Thus it was necessary to convey treasuries of African stories, history, and folklore by way of oral traditions.

MEDIA

Although freedom of the press is guaranteed in the constitution, in reality it remains restricted. The press consists of many weeklies, dailies, and other periodicals, and this sector has certainly become livelier since the 1990s. Almost all publications are in French and are issued in Abidjan. There are nine daily newspapers all told, and four of them are more widely read than the rest—*Fraternité Matin*, owned by the government, *Le Jour*, *La Nouvelle République*, and *La Voie*.

Radio is one of the most popular media in Côte d'Ivoire. Several radio stations exist, broadcasting in French and in the various African languages.

Ivorian men like to carry their radios with them.

There is a tier of low-power, noncommercial community radio stations, including some run by the Catholic Church. These include Radio Espoir, an Abidjan Catholic station, and Radio Paix Sanwi, an Aboisso Catholic station. Rebels in the center of the country use both radio and television facilities in Bouaké for their broadcasts. In 2005 UN peacekeepers launched their own radio station, Onuci FM, to broadcast programs that promote peace and reconciliation. This was initially available only in Abidjan but has since extended its reach to cover the rebel-held towns in the north.

As well as the newspaper *Fraternité Matin*, the government owns two major radio stations, and the only two national television channels in Côte d'Ivoire, La Première and TV 12. Only the government radio and television stations are broadcast nationwide. There are, however, pay-TV services, which are provided by Canal Satellite Horizons, a private enterprise.

While the independent stations have control over their editorial content, the government exercises considerable pressure over the media to promote government policies. Much of the news is devoted to the activities of the president, the government, and the Ivorian Popular Front (FPI) political party.

The government-owned newspapers rarely have any policy criticisms in their pages. Despite significant restrictions, independent and opposition newspapers frequently voice their disapproval of government actions. It is a crime to defame the president, prime minister, foreign chiefs of state or their diplomatic representatives, or state institutions. In 1991 a commission was set up to enforce laws against publishing material "undermining the reputation of the nation or defaming institutions of the State." In August 1995 the editor of the daily paper *Le Populaire* was arrested after the publication of an article alleging abuse of power by a public prosecutor. The article included a photo of an internal document, and the editor was charged with possession of a controlled government document. In the same year three opposition party journalists were convicted of publishing an article attributing the poor performance of an Ivorian soccer team to the president's presence at the international match. With the quite real threat of a jail sentence, journalists are extremely careful what they write.

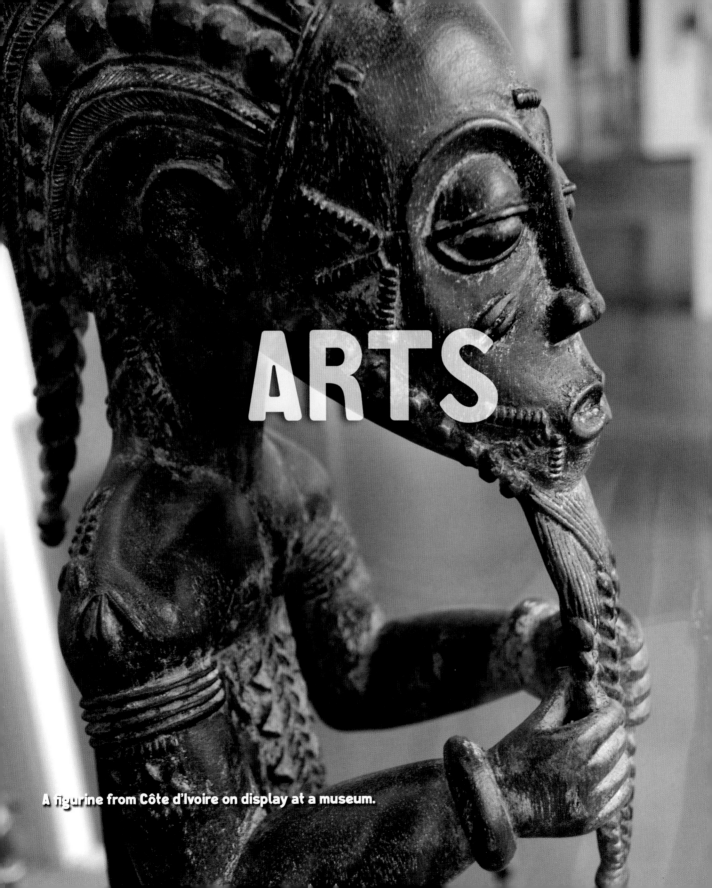

ARTS

A figurine from Côte d'Ivoire on display at a museum.

IVORIAN ART IS UNIQUE AND IS of great significance throughout the country. The family and ethnic groups are such crucial elements of life that all expressions of art serve to reinforce existing religious and social patterns.

Sculpture, masks, pottery, decorative textiles, and jewelry are examples of what Ivorian artists regularly create. The most popular materials used include wood, fiber, ivory, clay, earth, stone, and silver and gold. There is a functional purpose behind every piece of traditional Ivorian art, usually having to do with religious matters or to invoke health, village harmony, and bountiful harvests.

INDIGENOUS CULTURE

Before Europeans arrived, numerous cultural influences from other parts of Africa had spread through Côte d'Ivoire as a result of the Saharan trade routes. When the French came, they brought their culture with them. Modern Ivorians are greatly influenced by European cultural usages, sometimes to the extent of rejecting traditional ones. Fortunately, with the rise in African nationalism, cultural revivals are occurring in all African countries. Côte d'Ivoire is no exception—here the government encourages and provides support to dance troupes, music groups, artists, writers, and even the museums. Thus a strong indigenous culture can assert its presence confidently.

The arts of Côte d'Ivoire are among the best in West Africa and are distinctive to each ethnic group. Three groups, the Baule, Dan,

Mask making and sculpture are the two most thoroughly enjoyed crafts in the country. Many different types of material are used to make masks, although the most popular are gold and silver. Ivorians enjoy carving wood statues, and sculptures using certain metals or stone are widely popular. Both statues and masks have religious meanings carved into them.

A Kulango mask.

and Senufo, stand out from the rest. A popular Dan carving is that of a large spoon for serving rice. These spoons typically have two legs resembling human legs. The Senufo carve ornate doors to protect their community's food supplies. The Baule sculpt vessels for oracular purposes.

MASKS AND STATUES

Masks and statues are used during dances, masquerades, and religious ceremonies. They are carved out of single blocks of wood and decorated with clay, shells, beads, ivory, or feathers.

Ivorian art, like all African art, is rooted in ancestor worship. A mask represents the permanent bond between a tribe and its ancestors and is valued for the tradition it represents. The belief is that both man and animal are parts of the natural order, and that man should experience a oneness with all things in the natural world. Since natural elements contain an inner energy, the masks and statues absorb this energy from the dead. They are "spirit traps," used to control spirits for the benefit of the living. Masks are also used to illustrate gender roles in interesting ways.

DIFFERENT TYPES OF MASKS

During the construction of an ancestral mask, sculptors carve facial and bodily features differently from those on masks used for entertainment. They adopt communally approved artistic codes, such as the use of white as the color of death or the rendering of animal forms to reinforce the message of the mask. For example, the lion signifies strength, the spider shows prudence, and horns express the moon and fertility.

The most common Dan mask is a human face, slightly abstract but with realistic features, a smooth surface, a pouting mouth, slit or large circular eyeholes, and a calm expression. The slit-eyed ones are regarded as feminine masks, and they are used to prevent women from seeing uncircumcised boys undergoing initiation into adulthood. Traditionally worn in commemorative ceremonies, Baule facial masks are very realistic and tend to portray living individuals who can be recognized easily by their facial scars or hairstyles.

The masks and figures made by the Senufo people are used in ceremonies organized to honor village life. Senufo masks are highly stylized—the most famous is the "fire spitter" helmet mask, which is a combination of the antelope, warthog, and hyena. Another is the warthog mask, made to exorcise evil spirits. Hornbill figures, in a variety of sizes and styles, are important because that bird was the mythological founder of the Senufo people and a symbol of fertility.

One hornbill figure in particular has a long, hooked beak touching a protruding abdomen, symbolizing the continuation of life into future generations. Hornbills are considered admirable because they mate for life and share in the raising of the young. The figures are worn on the head during dances and processions.

Dance masks are used in village masquerades at the end of harvest festivities. Totemic masks appear first, such as the elephant mask representing the totem of its wearer. The Gu mask, symbolizing a beautiful woman, is a principal mask in the masquerade. Portrait masks are the last to be seen. They are stylized portrait representations of social values. A good example is a face with eyes downcast and lips closed, which illustrates modest respect and composure.

INTERWEAVING MASKS, MUSIC, AND DANCE

Ivorian traditions have unified the masquerade, music, and dance as the symbolic continuation of creation and life. In the context of the masquerade, the mask has a deep cultural significance. It provides a visual representation of invisible spirits. Thus the masquerade often becomes the performance in which the divine, or ancestral, spirits intervene from behind the masks.

The musician's role is to invoke the spirit to enter the masquerader, after which the mask and dancer are considered sacred and not to be desecrated.

Before constructing a musical instrument, the maker must ritually present offerings to honor the ancestral spirits who are believed will reside in the instrument.

During the masquerade the masked dancer is granted a symbolic status, and any utterances that the dancer makes are believed to be coming from the ancestor or god that is now in possession of his body. In such a ritual, the supernatural becomes an actual presence, ready to intervene in the affairs of the living. Alternatively, the occasion may be used to subtly convey messages and reproaches to members of the community, which if delivered in a different context would provoke anger and hostility.

The musical instrument is crucial in reinforcing the idea that external forces are lurking nearby. As a rule, instruments are made according to the tastes and habits of the musician. The tuning of these instruments is subject to the language patterns of the musician's mother tongue, as are also the rhythms generated when they are played. The resonating space inside the completed instrument is believed to give fullness to the ancestral voices, and it is the musician's performance on particular instruments that enables the ancestors to reveal themselves through the moving bodies of the dancers.

A dancer's body is thus considered an instrument that can be played by a skilled musician. The dancer, who is knowledgeable in the language of the music, makes certain audible or physical responses to particular sounds and rhythms, thereby translating these sounds into a dialogue with the ancestor.

TRADITIONAL MUSIC

The country's traditional music is characterized by a series of melodies and rhythms occurring in harmony. It may seem monotonous to some people, but in fact, African rhythms contain influences from Western popular music such as jazz, blues, and even rock.

Music is used to transmit knowledge and values and for celebrating communal and personal events. Stages of a person's life are marked with music specific to adolescent initiation rites, weddings, ancestral ceremonies, and funerals. There are different kinds of music for women, men, young people, and hunters.

Traditional music involves the use of a large assortment of instruments that are made with local materials. Drums are among the most popular instruments used. They come in a number of shapes, such as cylindrical, kettle, and hourglass. Several materials, such as wood, gourds, and clay, are used to construct drum bodies. Membranes are made from the skins of reptiles, cattle, goats, and other animals. The beautiful drums provide many different musical voices.

Other important percussion instruments include clap sticks, bells, rattles, gourds, clay pots, xylophones, and the lamellaphone. The latter is a series of metal or bamboo strips mounted on a board. It is held in the hands or on the player's lap, and the free ends of the strips are plucked with the thumbs. Stringed instruments include the musical bow, lute, and harp. The flute, whistle, oboe, and trumpet are the wind instruments. Flutes are made from bamboo, reeds, wood, clay, or bones. Trumpets are made from corn stems from the savanna areas with a reed sliced from the surface of the stem at one end.

Historically, traditional music has been the prerogative of one esteemed social group, the griot. They played a crucial role as historians in the kingdoms

Traditional musicians performing with the *balafon* (*left*), the Ivorian xylophone, and the cylindrical calabash (*right*).

To the Ivorians, music is an integral part of life, and it is said that each of them has a unique rhythm to which they must dance, summoned by the words embedded in these rhythms.

Important types of drums include drum-chimes in which a set of drums tuned to a scale is mounted in a frame and played by a team of drummers; friction drums, in which a sound is produced by rubbing the membrane; and the hourglass-shaped tension drum.

Drum ensembles consisting of three to five musicians who play connecting patterns are common. In the ensemble, each drummer uses a special method of striking the drumhead to produce varying pitches to distinguish his drum from all the others. Such ensembles often include rattles and an iron bell, which is struck with a drumstick to produce a repeated pattern called a time line.

Ivorian drummers play a critical role at ceremonies in which the gods enter the bodies of devotees. The skilled drummer must know many dozens of specific rhythms for particular gods and be responsible throughout the performance for monitoring the flow of supernatural powers.

that developed from the 10th century to the 20th century across Africa as a whole and Côte d'Ivoire in particular. At some time, griots became the official musicians of society. They played only instruments they could make themselves with local materials such as gourds, animal skins, and horns.

The griot's ancient art is still practiced today, though some say it has declined under the pressures of modern society. Today, families generally cannot afford their own private griot, so the musicians move from family to family, performing at weddings, baptisms, and other celebrations, entertaining and praising the guests. To experience their enduring power, a listener can turn on the radio or the television or attend a music festival.

Walking along a residential street, a traditional wedding may be encountered. A crowd of nicely dressed men and women will be gathered in the dirt street around a group of musicians playing through cranked-up amplifiers. There may be guitars, *balafon* (BAH-lah-fon, a wooden xylophone), or kora (a 21-string cross between a harp and a lute), all weaving a web of intricate melodies. Leading the entertainment will be a female griot singer in a fabulous embroidered gown, singing her heart out. Griots sing in loud, proud resonant voices full of the grandeur of their historic status. Their vocal styles reflect the influence of Islam on the music of the savanna region. The great majority of these beloved and honored vocalists are women. Guests will circulate before her, and if she praises them by name, they will happily give her money.

POPULAR MUSIC

Ivorian popular music is an amazing blend of African, European, American, and Middle Eastern traditions. It evolved from musicians and others who came to this country during the 20th century. Ballads were introduced during that time, and sailors from all over the world exposed the Ivorians to accordions and stringed instruments such as guitars. The subsequent development of popular music has been powerfully influenced by electronic mass media and the growing popularity of African music in the international music scene of the late 20th century.

An internationally renowned Ivorian artiste is Alpha Blonde. He was born in 1953 and now resides in New York. His music is strongly influenced by

Ivorian reggae star Tiken Jah Fakoly during a performance.

Young musicians have successfully created and made popular a new style of music, the Afrobeat, which is a mix of traditional African music with black American music.

Jamaican reggae, and he sings in his native language of Dioula as well as in French and in English. His lyrics convey strong political attitudes and a fine sense of humor.

TRADITIONAL DANCE

Dance is as varied in style and function as music. Dancing is associated with both sacred and secular events, and it plays a crucial role in education, work, entertainment, politics, and religious ritual. Common dance patterns include team dances using formations; group dances that invite individuals to showcase their skills; and solo dances, often performed by a professional entertainer. Body postures in Ivorian dance are typically earth-oriented movements in which the performer bends the knees and inclines the torso forward from the hips.

Some of the well-known dances include the N'Goron dance, a graceful initiation dance by young Senufo girls wearing only grass skirts and shell and

Priestesses of fetish magic dancing in a courtyard. Dancing is an important part of traditional religious rituals in long-established clans.

An artist hand painting a section of *korhogo* cloth.

feather headdresses, and the panther dance, which illustrates the courage, agility, and strength of the Senufo tribesman in his mastering of a hostile environment. It is usually performed when boys return from the Poro cult training encampment. The Koutouba and Kouroubissi dances are performed by Malinke women during the week before Ramadan.

TEXTILES

The Ivorians consider textiles and the decorative arts used in textiles as works of art and as significant social communication between family members. In particular, the art of making *korhogo* cloth is a tradition that is handed down from one generation to another. *Korhogo* cloth is a fabric woven by Senufo weavers that is then hand painted. The intricate symbols and patterns skillfully drawn on the cloth are evidence of their mastery of the traditional art of making textiles. The cloth is recognizable by the bold figures, usually

dark brown or black, painted on plain cotton material, usually white.

Korhogo craftsmen cooperate in an organized manner. The cotton spinning and dyeing are done by women, and the weaving is handled by men. The dye used for hand painting on the cloth is a mixture extracted from the bark and leaves of a shrub. It is used to draw mostly geometric figures and animal motifs such as chickens, lizards, and snakes. Traditionally, the decorated material was used by young people being initiated and by hunters and dancers.

JEWELRY

Jewelry is important to both Ivorian men and women. There are many types of jewelry. Beads are used to create objects that represent spiritual values, and such objects play major roles in community events such as birth, marriage, and death. Most common are the glass beads worn by village chiefs and elders as emblems of their power and wealth. Other materials used for making beads include coral, shells, silver, and gold. Gold and silver are precious and are sold by the gram. Necklaces that ward off evil are characterized by protective symbolism and are made in various designs. Some incorporate circle or fertility designs for both sexes, while other patterns may represent animal tracks, denoting power and cunning. Rings, earrings, and bracelets vary in style and symbolic content.

Shell headdresses are popular because it is believed that they can ward evil away.

LITERARY ARTS

Côte d'Ivoire's most famous and prolific writer is Bernard Dadié, whose work has been widely translated. One of his novels, *Climbié* (1971), is an autobiographical account of a childhood journey to France. Other translated works are *The Black Cloth* and *The City Where No One Dies*. Other well-known national novelists include Aké Loba and Ahmadou Kourouma. Loba is best known for *Kocoumbo*, an autobiographical novel of a young African's suffering the effects of being uprooted and poverty-stricken in Paris, who is drawn toward militant communism. Kourouma's best-selling novel, *The Suns of Independence*, tells the story of a village chief deposed after independence, losing his subjects, and having to adjust to a different life. The national library is located in Abidjan and so is a museum housing a variety of artistic, ethnographic, and scientific collections.

A girl reading the award winning *Aya de Yopougon* comic series by Ivorian Marguerite Abouet.

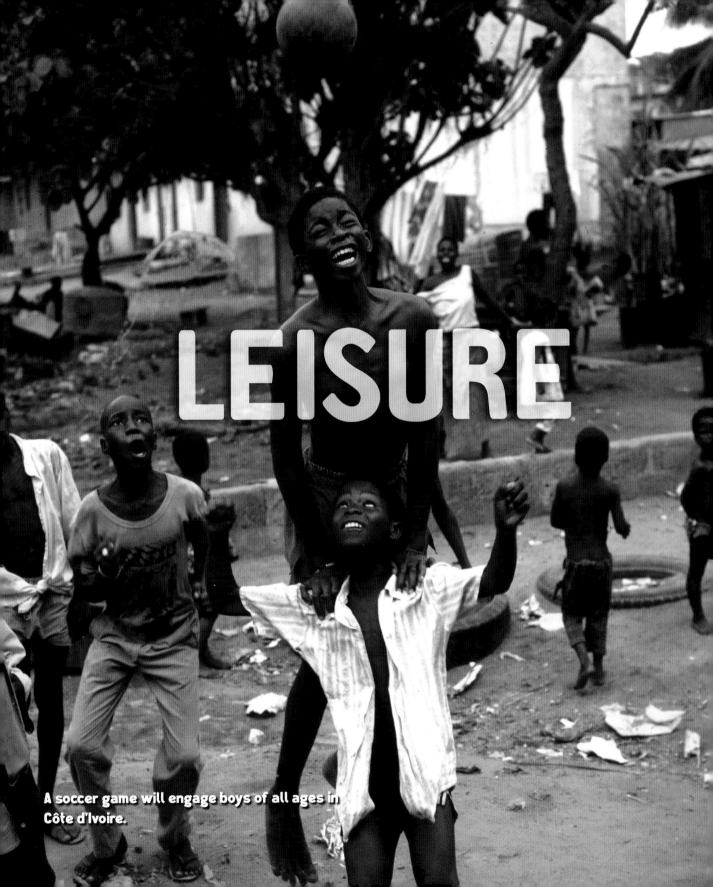

LEISURE

A soccer game will engage boys of all ages in Côte d'Ivoire.

FOR THE MAJORITY OF THE IVORIANS, who work hard all year, the Western concept of leisure is somewhat alien. Rather than resting and relaxing during their free time, the Ivorians, after finishing their chores, happily participate in the many communal events and celebrations of village life.

Free times that are not filled with activity are usually spent with friends of the same sex, playing board games, talking, and exchanging ideas.

Ivorian boys playing foosball, also called table soccer, at a market.

Just as it is in many African countries and throughout Europe, soccer is a major sport in Côte d'Ivoire. A soccer field will be found in almost every town and village, and there is at least one soccer club in every city. Some famous Ivorian soccer players include Didier Drogba, Salomon Kalou, and Emmanuel Eboue. Basketball and rugby— another type of football—are also widely played in the country.

Conveying ideas through storytelling is an enjoyable experience for all involved. There actually might be more free time for those who live and work in the towns and cities. The sandy beaches of Grand Bassam are favorite weekend getaways for them.

Sports are a popular pastime, especially among the men of Côte d'Ivoire, whether they are active players or simply spectators. Many often gather for a game among themselves when their work is done. Children are strongly encouraged to take up sports to build their bodies, increase their stamina, and to lead healthy lifestyles.

TRADITIONAL GAMES

Similar to backgammon, the game of *awale* (a-WA-lay) is an intellectual pastime enjoyed by Ivorians of all ages. It can be played by two people or by teams of more people. The rules are not difficult, but playing the game well takes a lot of practice. The *awale* board is rectangular, about 20 inches (51 cm) long, with two rows of six cups each. Game pieces are 48 peas or pebbles. There are several versions of the game, a variant of *mancala*, played by the different ethnic groups, but certain features are common in all versions.

To start the game, four peas are placed in each cup. The first player starts by picking up all the peas from any cup on his or her side of the board and dropping them one at a time in each consecutive cup to the right, counterclockwise. A person scores by capturing peas, and the winner is the one who captures the most peas. A person captures peas only when the last pea dropped falls in a cup on the opponent's side that contains only one or two peas. When that happens, the player picks up all the peas in that cup and sets them aside for counting at the end of the game.

STORYTELLING

Stories help people perceive who they are in relation to others and often aid in the understanding of a culture. Ivorian storytelling is full of wisdom, experience, and the teachings of a people who depended on an oral tradition

Even though some traditional stories can now be found in books, Ivorian parents still prefer to narrate them directly to their children because the storytelling hours greatly enrich their parent-child relationships.

One popular tale tells of a girl who gets lost in the woods and encounters a dirty and scruffy old woman. The old woman asks the girl to help clean her. The kindhearted girl agrees and is rewarded with a bowl that she is told to take home. The girl takes the bowl home and carefully places it in the house. The next day when she wakes up, the house is full of gold and silver! When the other villagers see this, they become very jealous. One woman tells her daughter to go to the woods and find this old woman.

The girl reluctantly does as she is told. When she meets the old woman, she refuses to help her. The old woman gives the girl three bowls anyway and tells her to throw the biggest one away, followed by the medium one. The small bowl is to be taken home. This greedy girl throws away the little one first, however, then the middle one, and takes the large one home. She thinks that the biggest bowl must contain the greatest amount of gold. The next day, instead of riches, she wakes up to find the house infested with disease, poverty, and unhappiness.

to pass stories, legends, and histories from one generation to another. These beloved accounts are powerful educational tools because they can teach the listeners some important lessons about traditional community life and values. Accompanied by music and sometimes dance, the stories can be about people, animals, or spirits, whether they are good or evil. The stories introduce their hearers to a world of knowledge, mystery, and magic that appeal to their emotions. Children love to listen to the stories their elders tell them. They often gather in a communal area for some enthralling stories when the elders are free to tell them.

SPORTS

Rugby is a popular sport in Côte d'Ivoire. There is a national team, and though relatively inexperienced, the members participate in the World Cup championship games. Basketball and softball are also widely played. There is a strong softball association in Abidjan to represent its interests. Golf can be played as Abidjan and Yamoussoukro each have good courses with grass greens. Because golf is such an expensive sport, the good courses are used mostly by tourists or businessmen. Locals are more likely to be seen on a less desirable green sand course made of sand and artificial fibers. Surfing, for those who can afford the expensive equipment, is available at the beaches. Most people opt to swim in pools found at the big hotels and in some of the main cities, as strong currents along the coast make swimming there dangerous.

Soccer is by far the nation's favorite sport. There are matches to watch every Sunday in the major cities. Unofficial games are always being played on the beach, in the streets, or at the university or municipal stadium. From an early age, boys are encouraged to take up the sport. The Ivorians are

Côte d'Ivoire's national soccer team celebrates its World Cup qualification.

proud of their national soccer team, nicknamed Les Éléphants (The Elephants). The national team is controlled by the Fédération Ivoirienne de Football. Until recently, their greatest accomplishment was winning the 1992 African Cup of Nations against Ghana. In October 2005 they qualified for the 2006 FIFA World Cup, marking their first appearance on the sport's greatest stage. Unfortunately, they were unable to qualify for the second round after losing to more experienced teams such as Argentina and Holland. There are also a number of Ivorian soccer players who play in internationally renowned football clubs. One such player is Didier Drogba, who plays for Chelsea, an English Premier League club.

OTHER ENTERTAINMENT

With adults, dancing is very popular. There are many places to go dancing, and dancing to a live African band is possible every night except Sundays for as little as a $6 entrance fee. Discotheques are the favorite entertainment spots for younger people. On weekends, these lively clubs become very crowded.

Ivorians enjoying a pickup game of basketball.

Movie theaters attract large audiences, too, with three to four showings a day in big cities such as Yamoussoukro and Bouaké. Most city people can afford this cheap but enjoyable diversion.

There is an ice-skating rink, a swimming pool, a bowling alley, and a movie theater in the biggest hotel in Abidjan, Hotel Ivoire. The rink is advertised as the only one in all of West Africa. It is an expensive recreation, however, restricted to urban teenagers who can afford to pay the high rink fees. In the capital, horseback riding is a popular avocation. Several riding clubs organize excursions to the forests and seaside.

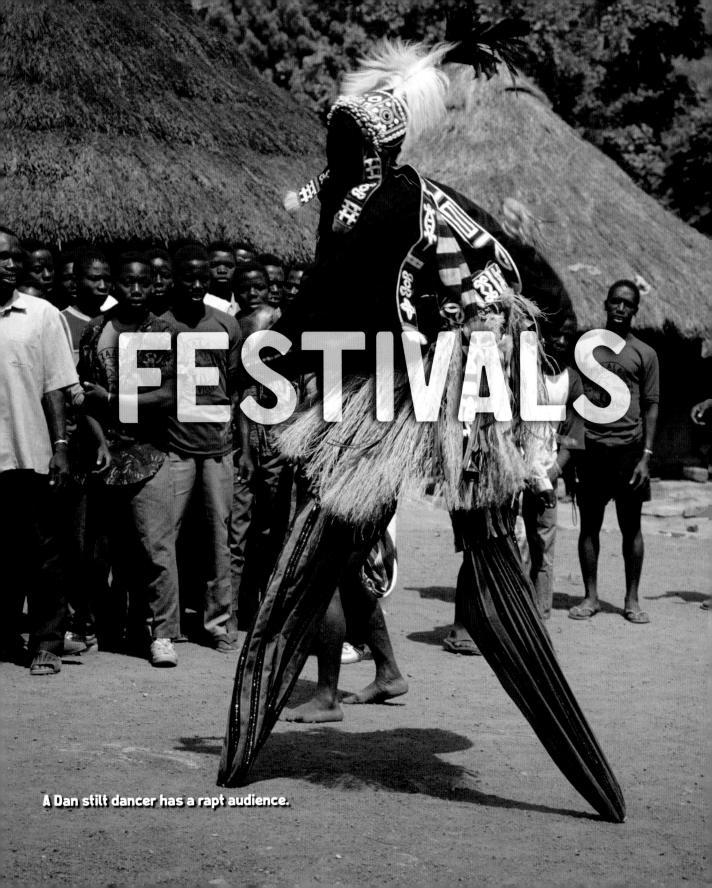

FESTIVALS

A Dan stilt dancer has a rapt audience.

VORIANS CELEBRATE MANY FESTIVALS throughout the year, most of which are closely tied to their religions. These festivals are usually a time to commemorate their Christian, Islamic, or traditional gods. Besides religious occasions, secular holidays also occupy a big part of the local festivities calendar.

CHRISTIAN HOLIDAYS

The Ivorians celebrate several Christian holidays. Easter, which celebrates the resurrection of Jesus Christ, is usually in April.

Street vendors trying to sell Christmas trees to motorists.

The Festival of Masks, or Fête des Masques, is one of the most popular festivals of the region. It is celebrated in November, and during this time many small villages hold competitions to select the best mask dancer, while prudently paying homage to the forest spirits who are personified in these masks.

Ascension Day, the rising of Christ into heaven on the fortieth day after the resurrection, is celebrated in May. Whitsunday falls on the seventh Sunday after Easter. This festival commemorates the descent of the Holy Spirit on the day of Pentecost. Assumption Day, the reception of Our Lady into heaven, is in August. All Saints' Day on November 1 honors loved ones who have died. Christmas Day celebrates the birth of Jesus Christ.

ISLAMIC CELEBRATIONS

Muslims observe Ramadan, which is the ninth month of the Islamic lunar calendar. During the month of Ramadan, Muslims fast between sunrise and sunset. According to the fourth pillar of Islam, fasting brings one closer to Allah. The discipline of fasting reminds Muslims of people who are deprived of life's basic necessities and the sufferings of less fortunate people. It also encourages Muslims to show compassion and kindness toward people in need.

Muslims from the Abobo quarter gather to pray during Eid al-Adha, the Feast of the Sacrifice.

Ramadan ends with a huge feast, called the Feast of Breaking the Fast, or Eid al-Fitr, which follows the sighting of the new moon. It is a joyous occasion when everyone prays together, visits friends and relatives, exchanges gifts, and eats lots of very good food. In many ways it is similar to the spirit of the American Thanksgiving. On Eid al-Fitr, Muslims express thanks for health, strength, and the opportunities in life given to them by Allah. Although the celebration lasts for 2 to 10 days, depending on the region, the main activities occur on the first day, the new moon.

The festival begins with a special prayer performed in a mosque. After the prayer, people greet each other warmly and give presents to the children. Then they visit relatives and friends, and everyone asks for forgiveness for any wrongdoings in the previous year.

The Feast of the Sacrifice, Eid al-Adha, starts on the 10th day of the last month of the Islamic calendar. This is also the month of pilgrimage to Mecca. The feast is especially meaningful to those who have made the pilgrimage. On that morning, Muslims assemble at a communal place of prayer, usually an open field, to pray together. After prayers, the head of each household sacrifices a sheep, a camel, or an ox for his family.

The man faces Mecca and calls out the names of the people on whose behalf the sacrifice is being made. Then he says, "In the name of Allah who is the Almighty," and in one stroke cuts the throat of the animal with a very sharp knife. The sacrificed animal is divided into three portions—the first one for the family, the second for relatives and friends, and the third share for the poor and needy.

TRADITIONAL FESTIVALS

THE FESTIVAL OF MASKS, or Fête des Masques, is celebrated annually in the Man villages each February. Each village in Man uses several masks and dances for this festival. Two famous dances are the stilt dance and the jugglers' dance.

The stilt dance is a unique dance performed by a group of young, masked Dan men. During their three to five years of training the dancers are instructed not to tell anyone, not even their wives, what they are doing. After their training, they can communicate with the spirits, who direct the dancers' complex acrobatic stunts during the strenuous performance.

Every village in the west has its own version of the jugglers' dance. Typically, a drumroll introduces the performers. This is followed with a dance by the guardian mask to exorcise evil spirits. Then young men armed with sharp daggers juggle 10-year-old girls in the air and catch them adroitly while holding the daggers but without ever cutting the girls. The girls wear skirts made of grass and headdresses decorated with cowrie shells.

THE FEAST OF DIPRI, or Fête du Dipri, takes place in April in Gomon, 62 miles (100 km) northwest of Abidjan. This is the home of the Abidji, the local ethnic group. The entire village stays awake all night within the safety of their huts. Around midnight, naked women and children sneak out of their huts to carry out nocturnal rites to cleanse the village of evil spells. Before sunrise, the chief appears, calling out to his people, "Chase out the evil."

The village men then emerge from their homes screaming out these same words. Drums pound, and the villagers slip into trances. Bodies squirm in the dust, everybody's eyes roll up into their sockets, and young people beat themselves and the ground with sticks. The frenzy continues until noon, when magic exercises begin. These exercises are initiation rituals for the young Abidji men. With sharp daggers, the initiates cut their stomachs. The men are not much hurt as their wounds heal quickly after being smeared with a balm concocted by medicine men. No one may enter the village of Gomon on the festival day itself.

YAM FESTIVALS are celebrated at the beginning and end of harvests with music, dances, and masquerades. The yam is such an integral part of the people's diet that a good harvest makes a great difference in their lives. The Ivorians take this opportunity, therefore, to honor the ancestors and spirits who protect their crops and to invite their good graces.

For the Agni and Baule people, the yam festival starts with the *anaya* (a-NAI-ya), a food offering to the gods, on the third Friday in October.

After the *anaya*, festivities are stopped for one month. At that time a memorial service is conducted for those who have died, and a purification rite is enacted to rid the village of evil influences. During the celebration a purification bundle, which includes a shoot of oil palm tree, a bush rope, and branches of the *atiz-dize* tree, is prepared. In the evening the bundle is carried aloft in a procession and then buried with prayers that no evil will cross the site. Farmers then carry in the new yam crop, and everyone tastes the fruits of the harvest.

For the Abron people, the yam festival is also a time to commemorate their arrival in Côte d'Ivoire from the east. The event is lavish with the enthroned king presiding over the festivities. He is dressed in a richly embroidered toga, wears a gold tiara, and holds in his right hand a solid gold scepter. He is covered by a huge scarlet canopy. All around him are his subjects in bright costumes, sitting under colorful umbrellas.

To observe the yam festival, Kulango parents and children exchange gifts and eat a meal of mashed yams and soup. Dances and singing are part of the celebrations.

SECULAR HOLIDAYS

NATIONAL DAY, held on December 7, commemorates the country's independence from France in 1960. Ivorians celebrate this happy occasion with traditional processions, dances, and music. Festivities are held throughout the country, but the biggest is in Yamoussoukro, the birthplace of Félix Houphouët-Boigny, the first president. On this day, the Guests Palace, an official residence for the president's guests, and City Hall are ablaze with many lights. Thousands of people attend the grand parade in Yamoussoukro.

NEW YEAR'S DAY is a time to celebrate the renewal of the natural order. It is also a time when all the ethnic groups hold masquerade parties. An important mask used in the celebrations is the plank mask, or *bedu* (BER-dew), which represents a wild animal that has been tamed by the mask.

For some clans, crops other than yams may be just as important. For example, the Dan people rely heavily on rice as a staple. If a rice harvest is good, young Dan girls will perform a dance of homage to the spirits protecting the crops.

FOOD

A shopper selecting chillis at the Adjema market.

F OOD IS A FASCINATING ASPECT of Ivorian culture. Many dishes are spicy, but there are plenty that are mild. The best eating places are at an Ivorian's home or at the plentiful food stalls on street corners.

EATING STYLES

In the Ivorian society, eating is not simply a matter of sustaining the body but an expression of the community spirit. The tradition is for all the

A colorful display of fresh produce at a Korhogo marketplace.

people in a village to eat together in a common area. The villagers are divided into three groups—women and girls eat as one group, men as another, and young boys as the third. Food is served in large containers and placed on mats on the ground. There is no need for utensils, as the Ivorians use their clean right hands to scoop up food instead of knives and forks. Usually a handful of rice is taken and formed into a ball along with some meat and sauce. After the meal, a washbasin is passed around.

Great piles of peppers on sale at a market.

FAVORITE FOODS

Chicken and fish are the favorite foods of Ivorians. For many, however, eating meat is restricted by its high cost and inaccessibility. Thus vegetables make up a large part of an Ivorian's diet and provide for significant amounts of vitamins. A typical meal includes a staple, such as rice or cassava, and a sauce in which to dip the rice. Leafy vegetables, root crops, and hot peppers are commonly boiled or added to soups and stews. Ivorians typically do not eat a dessert, but sometimes fresh fruit is served after a meal.

The right hand is used for making the ball of food and for eating because of the long-standing practice of using the left hand to cleanse one's body.

HOT PEPPERS originated in South America. Today they are a staple in Côte d'Ivoire where several varieties are cultivated for local use. There are many kinds of hot peppers of interesting colors and shapes and with varying degrees of hotness. Habanero, a type of hot pepper, is more widely cultivated than any other variety and is one of the hottest. The fruit of the habanero has a smoky flavor and is usually red or yellow. Ivorians use habanero to spice up virtually every dish on the table, because its smoky aroma adds a familiar special taste to soups, stews, and sauces.

YAMS are widely cultivated in Côte d'Ivoire. Both the leaves and the root are eaten. The leaves are steamed and cooked in palm oil with okra, lima beans, hot peppers, and smoked fish, and usually served with rice. The roots may be peeled and boiled or used to make French fries. Yams can range in color from yellow to orange-red to purple, and can be classified into two types—dry or moist. Dry yams have a powdery texture after cooking. Yams are often added to onions and tomatoes and sautéed with peppers. The mixture is boiled until the yams are soft.

OKRA is another widely grown plant. A typical okra can grow up to 6 feet (1.8 m) tall. The leaves are lobed and are generally hairy. The plant first produces dark yellow flowers and then pods, which are the edible portions of the plant. Young pods are thinly sliced to prepare okra soup. Tough and fibrous pods are dried and then ground into a powder, which is used for thickening stews. Fresh young pods can be dried for use anytime in soups.

Okra pods are favorite soup ingredients.

ALOCO *(AL-oh-ko)* *is ripe bananas cooked in palm oil and garnished with steamed onions and chilies. It can be eaten alone or with grilled fish.*

ATTIÉKÉ *(AT-tee-eck-eh)* *is a popular side dish of grated cassava. Attiéké is like couscous, which is a dish of prepared wheat pellets steamed over broth with meat or fruit added, prevalent in many parts of Africa. In Côte d'Ivoire, it is made with cassava.*

KEDJENOU *(KED-gen-ooh)* *is chicken cooked with different kinds of vegetables in a mild sauce. It is cooked in a clay pot over a low fire or wrapped in banana leaves and buried in hot wood ashes. This dish can be served with yams, attiéké, or rice.*

N'VOUFOU *(FOO-fue)* *is mashed bananas or yams mixed with palm oil and served with eggplant sauce.*

FOUTOU *(FOO-too)* *is made by boiling cassava and bananas until cooked. The cassava and banana are then separately pounded, with drops of water added from time to time to avoid sticking and to bring them to the desired consistency. Then they are mixed together and pounded again, with a little salt added for taste.*

Cassava is a tropical perennial plant introduced by Portuguese sailors returning from Brazil in the 16th century.

CASSAVA, also known as tapioca, is divided into sweet and bitter types. Ivorians enjoy the cassava as a daily staple, like rice, because it is nutritious and grows easily under a variety of conditions. Both the roots and leaves are edible. Cooking the cassava can be an arduous task because the root contains cyanide, a potentially poisonous salt. Only after grating, squeezing out the liquid, and cooking is the cassava is safe to eat.

EGGPLANT has erect or spreading branches bearing egg-shaped white or beautiful dark purple fruit. It is cooked in the same way as other vegetables.

BEVERAGES

Ivorians enjoy drinking ginger beer, a soft drink made with a lot of ginger, almost enough to burn the throat. To make ginger beer, about 1 pound of peeled and mashed gingerroot and an unpeeled pineapple are added to about 2 quarts (1.89 liters) of boiling water. Lime juice, raisins, or guava may also be used. The mixture is left to stand overnight. The next day it is strained to remove the fruit, sugar is added, and the drink is chilled.

Although not many Ivorians drink beer, except those living along the coast, there is a good local brew called Flag. A homemade drink is *bangui* (BAN-kee), a local white palm wine. Yeast is added to the juice tapped from a palm tree, and the mixture is left to ferment overnight. Soft drinks are the most popular beverages among women and youth who do not drink alcohol.

Ivorian fans celebrate Côte d'Ivoire's World Cup qualification with popular local drinks.

POPULAR EATING SPOTS

The cities have many restaurants, and Abidjan in particular has eating places serving French, Italian, Caribbean, Lebanese, and Vietnamese food. There are a growing number of establishments catering to non-Africans who want to sample traditional local food. Among them, the *maquis* eateries are the most popular. They are inexpensive outdoor cafés with chairs and tables or wooden benches and sometimes a sandy floor, and are found almost everywhere throughout the country. Popular dishes in a *maquis* include braised chicken or fish with onions and tomatoes, *attiéké*, and *kedjenou*. To be considered a *maquis*, braised food—slow cooked with a little moisture—must be available. A *maquis* usually opens only in the evenings.

At lunchtime in the cities, waitresses set up stands outside established restaurants to serve rice or *foutou* with various sauces. Patrons make their choices from delicacies such as fish sauce or gumbo sauce, and then go inside to eat. This service is especially useful for the busy urbanites who drop by for a quick tasty lunch.

THE FOOD CRISIS

Food is more than just a base necessity in Côte d'Ivoire. It incorporates a lifestyle that defines community spirit. Unfortunately, the world was severely impacted by the food crisis of 2007 to 2008. Those two years saw a dizzying increase in food prices, igniting a global emergency and bringing on political and economic instability and social unrest in poor and undeveloped nations. There are several factors said to have caused the crisis, such as bad weather resulting in poor yields; the heightened cost of fertilizers, food transportation, and industrial agriculture; as well as growing consumer demands across the expanding middle-class populations in Asia. Some observers have even said that the food crisis stems from unprecedented global population growth. World population has, after all, skyrocketed from 1.6 billion in 1900 to an estimated 6.7 billion today. This had led to the universal challenge of producing enough food for the ever expanding population in the shortest amount of time and with the world's limited resources.

Some of the worst instability resulting from high food costs has been felt in West Africa. One person was killed and dozens were injured as riots tore through Côte d'Ivoire after the prices of meat and wheat increased by 50 percent within a week. President Laurent Gbagbo was forced to cut taxes to deal with the turbulence. Violent protests also broke out in Cameroon, Burkina Faso, and Senegal.

Although the food crisis is far from over, the global community continues to act together to find resolutions to the tough situation. The UN has also created a high-level task force to bolster cooperation, particularly between developing nations.

A resident buying grain at the Abobo market. Rising food costs brought about economic and social instability in the country.

KEDJENOU

Traditionally *kedjenou* is slow-cooked in a large earthenware jar with a narrow neck that is usually placed directly over a wood fire. If it is being cooked out in the bush, the food is securely wrapped in a banana leaf and placed under hot ashes. This recipe can be adapted to a deep oven casserole, a Dutch oven on top of the stove, or a slow cooker.

3½ pounds (1½ kg) chicken

1 eggplant, peeled and cut into small pieces

2 large onions, finely chopped

2 fresh red or green hot peppers, seeded and cut into strips

4 tomatoes, peeled, seeded, and finely crushed

1 small piece of gingerroot, peeled and grated

1 sprig thyme

1 bay leaf

Salt to taste

Rinse the chicken well and cut into pieces. Place it in the cooking vessel with the eggplant, onions, peppers, tomatoes, ginger, thyme, bay leaf, and salt. Hermetically seal the jar, if using the traditional vessel, by tying a banana leaf around the collar so that air does not escape, or cover the pot with a tight-fitting lid. No moisture should escape. No water needs to be added during cooking. If cooking traditionally, place the jar on hot coals and cook for about 45 minutes. Or place over a low flame or in a 350°F (176°C) oven for about the same time. In a slow cooker, cook on low-heat setting for 6 to 7 hours or on high-heat setting for 3 to 3½ hours. During cooking occasionally raise the cooking vessel and shake it vigorously so that the food does not stick to the bottom.

MANGO FOOL

Ivorians generally do not eat dessert, although they do have a selection of fruit after dinner on occasion. As such, if and when they do indulge in an after-meal dessert, it is usually a simple dish, much like the mango fool.

10 very ripe mangoes, peeled

6 teaspoons (30 milliliters) Cointreau (an aperitif) or orange juice

1 cup (250 ml) heavy cream

Mint sprigs for garnishing

Extract all the flesh from the mangos, including the flesh inside the skin and around the seeds. Place the flesh into a blender together with the Cointreau or juice and the cream. Blend the mixture for about 30 to 45 seconds, until cream is thickened. Pour the mixture into a large dessert bowl or individual dessert glasses. Allow the mixture to cool in the refrigerator until it sets. Decorate the fool with mint sprigs before serving.

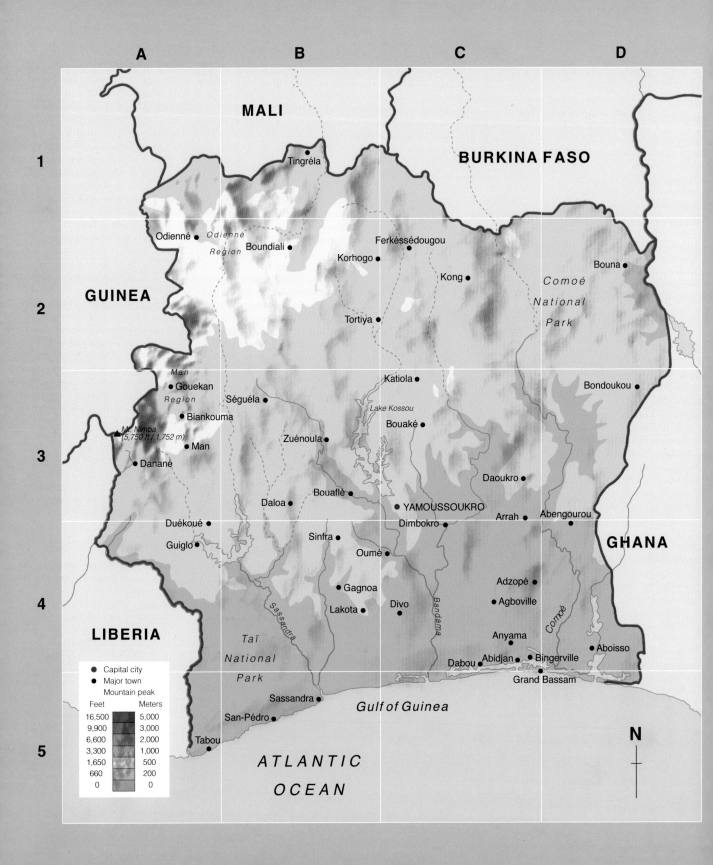

MALI

BURKINA FASO

1

Tingréla •

GUINEA

2

Odienné •   *Odienné Region*   Boundiali •

Ferkéssédougou •

Bouna •

Korhogo •

Kong •

Comoé National Park

Tortiya •

3

Man Region   • Gouekan

Séguéla •

Katiola •

Bondoukou •

• Biankouma

Lake Kossou

▲ Mt. Nimba
(5,750 ft / 1,752 m)

• Man

Zuénoula •

Bouaké •

Danané •

Daoukro •

Bouaflé •

YAMOUSSOUKRO •

Abengourou •

Daloa •

Arrah •

Duékoué •

Dimbokro •

4

Guiglo •

Sinfra •

GHANA

Oumé •

Adzopé •

Gagnoa •

Agboville •

LIBERIA

Lakota •

Divo •

Bandama

Sassandra

Anyama •

Comoé

Aboisso •

Taï National Park

Dabou • Abidjan • Bingerville •

Grand Bassam •

Sassandra •

5

San-Pédro •

Gulf of Guinea

Tabou •

N

ATLANTIC OCEAN

• Capital city
• Major town
▲ Mountain peak

Feet	Meters
16,500	5,000
9,900	3,000
6,600	2,000
3,300	1,000
1,650	500
660	200
0	0

MAP OF CÔTE D'IVOIRE

Abengourou, D4
Abidjan, C4
Aboisso, D4
Adzopé, C4
Agboville, C4
Anyama, C4
Arrah, C3
Atlantic Ocean, A5,
    B5, C5, D5

Bandama River, C4
Biankouma, A3
Bingerville, C4
Bondoukou, D3
Bouaflé, B3
Bouaké, C3
Bouna, D2
Boundiali, B2
Burkina Faso, C1,
    D1

Comoé National
    Park, C2, D2
Comoé River,
    C2—C3, D3—D4

Dabou, C4
Daloa, B3
Danané, A3
Daoukro, C3
Dimbokro, C4
Divo, C4
Duékoué, A4

Ferkéssédougou, C2

Gagnoa, B4
Ghana, D1—D5
Gouekan, A3
Grand Bassam, C4
Guiglo, A4
Guinea, A1—A3
Gulf of Guinea, B5,
    C5, D5

Katiola, C3
Kong, C2
Korhogo, B2

Lake Kossou, B3, C3
Lakota, B4
Liberia, A3—A5

Mali, A1, B1, C1
Man Region, A3
Man, A3
Mt. Nimba, A3

Odienné Region,
    A2, B2
Odienné, A2
Oumé, C4

San-Pédro, B5
Sassandra River,
    B4—B5
Sassandra, B5
Séguéla, B3
Sinfra, B4

Tabou, A5
Taï National Park,
    B4—B5
Tingréla, B1
Tortiya, B2

Yamoussoukro, C3

Zuénoula, B3

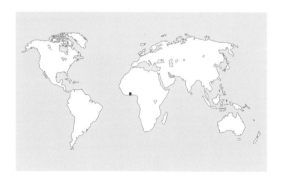

ECONOMIC CÔTE D'IVOIRE

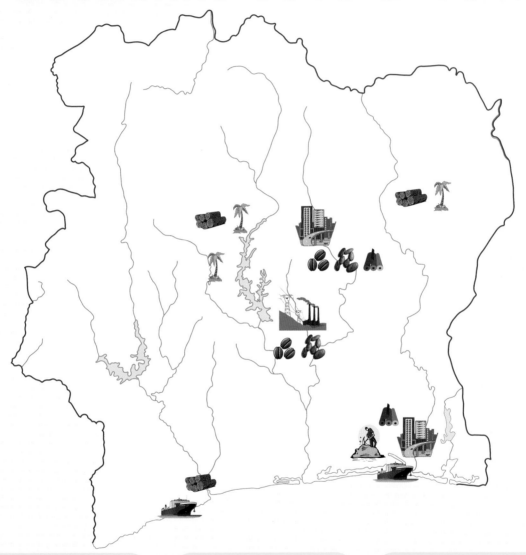

Agriculture

 Cocoa

 Coffee

Manufacturing

 Textiles

Services

 Cultural
& political center

 Power plant

 Ports

Natural Resources

 Mines

 Palm oil

 Timber

ABOUT THE ECONOMY

OVERVIEW

Agriculture is one of Cote d'Ivoire's main economic sectors and is responsible for about 60 percent of employment. The export of agricultural products, such as cocoa, coffee, and palm oil has also made the country one of the most economically successful among West African nations. The government has been seeking to diversify the economy and is looking into oil exploration and oil and gas production. However, the country's economic potential and growth has been undermined by civil unrest and political instability.

GROSS DOMESTIC PRODUCT (GDP)
$34.1 billion (2008 estimate)

ANNUAL GDP GROWTH
2.3 percent (2008 estimate)

ANNUAL GDP GROWTH PER CAPITA
$1,700 (2008 estimate)

STRUCTURE OF THE ECONOMY AS PERCENTAGEs OF GDP
Agriculture: 28; industry: 21.6; services: 50.4 (2008 estimate)

CURRENCY
African Financial Community franc (CFA)
US$1 = 455,890 CFA francs (January 2010)

EXPORTS
$10.09 billion (2008 estimate)

GROSS DOMESTIC SAVINGS
$18.1 billion

GROSS NATIONAL SAVINGS
$12.8 billion

POPULATION BELOW POVERTY LINE
43.2 percent

MAIN EXPORTS
Cocoa, coffee, tropical hardwoods, cotton, bananas, petroleum, pineapples, palm oil

MAIN IMPORTS
Food, consumer goods, capital goods, fuel, transportation equipment

CULTURAL CÔTE D'IVOIRE

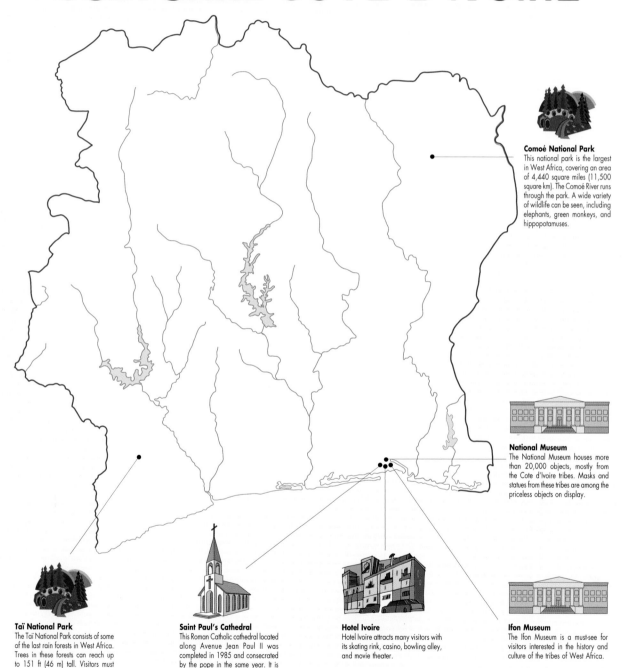

Comoé National Park
This national park is the largest in West Africa, covering an area of 4,440 square miles (11,500 square km). The Comoé River runs through the park. A wide variety of wildlife can be seen, including elephants, green monkeys, and hippopotamuses.

National Museum
The National Museum houses more than 20,000 objects, mostly from the Cote d'Ivoire tribes. Masks and statues from these tribes are among the priceless objects on display.

Taï National Park
The Taï National Park consists of some of the last rain forests in West Africa. Trees in these forests can reach up to 151 ft (46 m) tall. Visitors must obtain a permit to visit the national park. Scientists have been carrying out research on chimpanzees in the area since the 1970s.

Saint Paul's Cathedral
This Roman Catholic cathedral located along Avenue Jean Paul II was completed in 1985 and consecrated by the pope in the same year. It is now an icon of Abidjan. Designed by Aldo Spiritom, the cathedral's tower is a stylized Saint Paul, with his robes trailing behind him.

Hotel Ivoire
Hotel Ivoire attracts many visitors with its skating rink, casino, bowling alley, and movie theater.

Ifon Museum
The Ifon Museum is a must-see for visitors interested in the history and culture of the tribes of West Africa.

ABOUT THE CULTURE

OFFICIAL NAME
République de Côte d'Ivoire

DATE OF INDEPENDENCE
August 7, 1960

NATIONAL FLAG
Three equal vertical bands of orange (hoist side), white, and green. Design based on the flag of France.

LAND AREA
124,504 square miles (322,463 square kilometers)

COASTLINE
320 miles (515 km)

CLIMATE
Tropical along coast, semiarid in far north

HIGHEST POINT
Mount Nimba (5,748 feet/1,752 m)

CAPITAL
Yamoussoukro

MAIN CITIES
Abidjan, Bouaké, Man, Korhogo, Bondoukou, San-Pédro

PORTS AND HARBORS
Abidjan, Aboisso, Dabou, San-Pédro

POPULATION
20.6 million (July 2009 estimate)

LIFE EXPECTANCY
55.44 years (2009 estimate)

MAJOR LANGUAGES
French (official language), Dioula, Senufo, Agni, Baule, Dan/Yacouba

MAJOR ETHNIC GROUPS
Akan 42.1 percent, Voltaiques or Gur 17.6 percent, Northern Mandes 16.5 percent, Krous 11 percent, Southern Mandes 10 percent, other 2.8 percent (includes 130,000 Lebanese and 14,000 French) (1998)

MAJOR RELIGIONS
Islam 38.6 percent, Christianity 32.8 percent, indigenous religions 11.9 percent, none 16.7 percent (2008 estimate)

FAMOUS POLITICAL LEADERS
Félix Houphouët-Boigny
Henri Konan-Bédié
Daniel Kablan Duncan

CURRENT POLITICAL LEADERS
President Laurent Gbagbo
Prime Minister Guillaume Soro

TIME LINE

IN CÔTE D'IVOIRE	IN THE WORLD
	323 B.C. Alexander the Great's empire stretches from Greece to India.
	1206–1368 Genghis Khan unifies the Mongols and starts conquest of the world. At its height, the Mongol Empire under Kublai Khan stretches from China to Persia and parts of Europe and Russia.
late 1400s Portuguese establish trading settlements along the coast.	**1789–99** The French Revolution
1893 Côte d'Ivoire becomes a French colony.	
1904 Côte d'Ivoire becomes part of the French Federation of West Africa.	**1914** World War I begins.
	1939 World War II begins.
1944 Félix Houphouët-Boigny founds the interterritorial African Democratic Rally and the Ivory Coast Democratic Party.	**1945** The United States drops atomic bombs on Hiroshima and Nagasaki.
1958 Côte d'Ivoire becomes a republic within the French Community.	
1960 France grants independence under nation's first president, Félix Houphouët-Boigny. He holds power until he dies in 1993.	
1990 Houphouët-Boigny wins first multiparty presidential elections.	**1986** Nuclear power disaster at Chernobyl in Ukraine
1993 Henri Konan-Bédié becomes president.	
1995 Bédié reelected in a ballot that is boycotted by opposition parties in protest at restrictions imposed on their candidates.	**1997** Hong Kong is returned to China.
1999 Alassane Ouattara, a Muslim, runs in presidential race splitting the country along ethnic and religious lines.	

IN CÔTE D'IVOIRE	IN THE WORLD
2000 After much controversy over rigged polls and calls for fresh elections, President Gbagbo's FPI emerges as the dominant single party in parliamentary elections.	
2001 Much political infighting and civil unrest. President Gbagbo sets up National Reconciliation Forum but clashes continue.	
2003 President Gbagbo accepts peace deal proposing power-sharing government. Military chiefs and rebels declare end of war.	**2003** War in Iraq begins.
2004 Deadly clashes during crackdown on opposition rally against President Gbagbo in Abidjan. UN Peacekeeping forces deployed.	**2004** Eleven Asian countries hit by giant tsunami, killing at least 225,000 people
2005 Economist Charles Konan Banny is nominated as prime minister by mediators.	**2005** Hurricane Katrina devastates the Gulf Coast of the United States.
2006 UN Security Council resolution extends the transitional government's mandate for another year.	
2007 Despite signing a power-sharing peace deal, violence continues. UN Security Council votes to maintain sanctions for another year. Rebel and government soldiers pull back from frontline positions as part of process to reunite country.	
2008 Date of long-awaited presidential elections rescheduled from June to November.	**2008** Earthquake in Sichuan, China, kills 67,000 people.
2009 The International Monetary Fund agrees to write off $3 billion of $12.8 billion national debt. Presidential election date is reset for early 2010.	**2009** Outbreak of flu virus H1N1 world pandemic

GLOSSARY

anaya (a-NAI-ya)
Offering of food to the gods during the yam festival.

attiéké (AT-tee-eck-eh)
Grated cassava dish.

awale (a-WA-lay)
Ivorian board game, a variant of mancala, similar to backgammon.

bedu (BER-dew)
Plank mask used in New Year's Day celebrations.

Eid al-Adha
Feast of the sacrifice that marks the end of the pilgrimage to Mecca.

Eid al-Fitr
Celebration of the breaking of the fast at the end of the Islamic month of Ramadan.

Fête des Masques
Festival of masks celebrated annually by the Dan people.

Fête du Dipri
Feast of Dipri celebrated by the Abidji.

gendarmerie
Branch of armed forces responsible for general law enforcement, a national police.

griot
Elite people entrusted with passing down oral tradition and cultural heritage to succeeding generations. Griots are historians, praise singers, and musical entertainers.

grisgris
Necklace amulet believed to ward off evil.

Hadith
Collection of Prophet Muhammad's sayings that supplements the Koran in guiding Muslims.

hajj
Muslim pilgrimage to Mecca.

kora
A 21-stringed musical instrument that is a cross between a harp and a lute.

marabous
Traditional religious leaders.

maquis (MA-kee)
Outdoor eating place for quick meals.

PDCI
Democratic Party of Côte d'Ivoire, the dominant political party in the country.

salat (sa-LAHT)
Muslim prayer.

SAVAC
Special Anti-Crime Police Brigade.

zakat (za-KAHT)
Islamic obligation of giving alms.

FOR FURTHER INFORMATION

BOOKS

Erdman, Sarah. *Nine Hills to Nambonkaha: Two Years in the Heart of an African Village*. NY: Picador, 2004

Habeeb, William Mark. *Ivory Coast* (Africa). Broomall, PA: Mason Crest Publishers, 2004.

Hudgens, Jim, Richard Trillo, and Nathalie Calonnec. *The Rough Guide to West Africa*. London, UK: Rough Guides Ltd. (Penguin), 2008.

Reed, Daniel B. *Dan Ge Performance: Masks and Music in Contemporary Cote d'Ivoire* (African Expressive Culture). Bloomington, IN: Indiana University Press, 2003.

WEBSITES

African Studies Center. Cote d'Ivoire page. www.africa.upenn.edu/Country_Specific/Cote. html

allAfrica.com. http://allafrica.com/cotedivoire/

Brother Ayouba. www.ayouba.com/

FIFA.com. www.fifa.com/worldcup/teams/team=43854/index.html

Friends of Côte d'Ivoire. www.friendsofcotedivoire.org/

United Nations Operation in Cote d'Ivoire. www.un.org/en/peacekeeping/missions/unoci/index.shtml

MUSIC

Best of Alpha Blondy (CD). Shanachie, 1990.

BIBLIOGRAPHY

BOOKS

Adou Yao and C. Y. Roussou. *Forest Management, Farmers' Practices and Biodiversity Conservation in the Monogaga Protected Coastal Forest in Southwest Côte d'Ivoire*. Bernard, UK: Edinburgh University Press, 2007.

Gottlieb, Alma and Phillip Graham. *Parallel Worlds*. New York: Crown Publishing, 1993.

Sandler, Bea. *The African Cookbook*. New York: Carol Publishing Group, 1993.

WEBSITES

ACCRA Declaration. Participants' Statement. ACCRA Declaration on Forest Law Compliance in West African Countries. http://illegal-logging.info/uploads/1_AccraDeclarationAug20E1.pdf

Agence France-Presse. "Ivory Coast Pollution Toll Surges Upward, Seven Arrested," September 12, 2006. http://Factiva.com/

Amnesty International. Côte d'Ivoire: Amnesty International Appeal to All Parties. www.amnesty.org/en/library/asset/AFR31/007/2000/en/f8fe6dc5-faaf-4abc-a63f-4b2368e6575a/afr310072000en.pdf

Country Profile: Ivory Coast. http://news.bbc.co.uk/2/hi/africa/country_profiles/1043014.stm

District of Yamoussoukro. Economic Perspectives. http://yamoussoukro.org

Encyclopaedia Britannica. Côte d'Ivoire—Economy. www.britannica.com/EBchecked/topic/139651/Cote-dIvoire/55127/Economy

IRIN News. Côte d'Ivoire: Civil War Allows Rampant Illegal Logging. www.irinnews.org/report.aspx?reportid=52512

Living Africa, The. National Parks, Taï National Park. http://library.thinkquest.org/16645/national_parks/ci_tnp.shtml

Monga Bay. Tropical Rain Forests: World Rain Forests (Côte d'Ivoire). http://rainforests.mongabay.com/20cotedivoire.htm

Rainforest Portal. Action Alert: Unilever Threatens Côte d'Ivoire's Primary Rainforests, Showing Promises of "Sustainable" Palm Oil Meaningless. http://rainforestportal.com/shared/alerts/send.aspx?id=ivory_coast_oil_palm

Relief Web. Political Agreement Signed in March Eased Tensions in Côte d'Ivoire, but Delays in Implementation Growing Concern, Security Council Told. www.reliefweb.int/rw/rwb.nsf/db900sid/EGUA-788S8A?OpenDocument

Trekearth, Côte d'Ivoire in Photos. www.trekearth.com/gallery/Africa/Cote_dIvoire/

U.S. Department of State. Background Note: Côte d'Ivoire. www.state.gov/r/pa/ei/bgn/2846.htm

World Bank. Côte d'Ivoire at a Glance. http://devdata.worldbank.org/AAG/civ_aag.pdf

INDEX

agriculture, 8, 11, 12, 45,
47—48, 48, 53, 56, 128
slash-and-burn, 12
arable land, 8
average annual rainfall, 10

beverages, 127
bilingual, 93
biodiversity, 55, 60
births, 76

carnivores, 12
cash crops, 19, 21, 48, 65
chores, 67, 75, 111
Christian holidays, 117—118
cities, 13—15
Abidjan, 14—15, 73
Bouaké, 15, 73
Yamoussoukro, 13—14
civil servants, 22
clan kingdoms, 17
climate, 9—10
communes, 29
conservation, 57, 59
constitution, 23, 29, 96
corruption, 37, 58
crime rate, 69
currency, 50
West African CFA franc, 50

dance, 66, 106—107
stilt dance, 119
debt, 45—46
debt payment, 22
deforestation, 8, 12, 55, 56, 73
democracy, 22, 41, 42, 43
desert
Sahara, 10, 17
distribution of wealth, 71
dress, 70—71
casual attire, 70—71
traditional dress, 70—71

economic growth, 22, 45
economic progress, 68, 71
ecosystems, 59
education, 75, 78—80

elections, 21, 22, 23, 24, 26, 29,
30, 31, 33, 43
electoral system, 31
energy, 51—52
electricity, 52
hydroelectric plants, 52
natural gas, 52
solar power, 52
entertainment, 115
environmental agreements
Accra Declaration, 59
environmental problems, 11, 56
Ethiopian biogeographic zone, 10
ethnic groups, 93
Abe, 19
Abron, 8, 64—65
Agni, 8, 64—65
Anyi, 19
Baule, 8, 19, 64
Dan (Yacouba), 66
Dioula, 66—67
Kru, 68—69
Kulango, 67—68
Lobi, 67
Senufo, 65—66
export growth, 45
exports, 19, 50
cocoa, 45, 47, 48, 50, 55
coffee, 45, 48, 50, 55
hardwood, 10, 49, 56
extinction, 12

family, 73—74
children, 75—76
farming, 12, 21, 55, 65, 74
fauna, 10—13
financial aid, 42
fishing, 68
flora, 10
folklore, 66
food crisis, 128—129
forced labor, 19, 20, 21, 27, 37
foreign relations, 22, 41—42
forests, 56—57
forest reserves, 57
Tanoé Swamps Forest, 58
freedom of assembly, 36—37

freedom of expression, 36—37
freedom of religion, 83
French colony, 14, 19
funerals, 76

games, 112
gendarmerie, 34, 35, 53
global warming, 56
griots, 67, 95, 104
gross domestic product, 47
guerrilla resistance, 19
Gulf of Guinea, 7, 8

health care, 80—81
HIV/AIDS, 42, 81
housing
apartment, 77
mud huts, 78
human rights abuse, 37—39
child labor, 39
child soldiers, 39
domestic violence, 39
human trafficking, 37
humid, 9

illegal logging, 57—59, 58
imports, 50
independence, 20—22
indigenous culture, 99—100
indigenous peoples, 19, 63—69
industrialization, 15
infrastructure, 51
initiation rites, 66, 102
insects, 13
investments, 45, 50
Islamic holidays
Eid al-Fitr, 119
Feast of the Sacrifice, 119
Ramadan, 118—119

jewelry, 108—109

Koran, 85, 86

labor force, 11, 53
labor code, 53
minimum wage, 53

INDEX

minimum working age, 52
unions, 53
working conditions, 52—53
language
    French, 93, 95
    spoken languages, 93—95
literacy, 77, 79, 80
literary arts, 109
living standards, 41

macroeconomic stability, 46
maps
    map of Côte d'Ivoire, 132
    cultural Côte d'Ivoire, 134
    economic Côte d'Ivoire, 136
malaria, 12
malnutrition, 81
manufacturing, 48—49
marriage, 74, 77
masks, 100—101, 121
masquerades, 100, 101, 101—102, 121
media, 96—97
men's roles, 76
migrants, 77
military, 34—36
mining, 49
multiparty parliamentary
    democracy, 22
music, 102—104
    popular music, 105—106

national parks, 9
    Comoé National Park, 9, 59
    Taï National Park, 9, 11, 57
natural resources, 10, 55, 58
nonhumanitarian aid, 42
Non-Ivorian Africans, 69—70

one-party regime, 22

peacekeeping troops, 24
places of worship
    Basilica of Our Lady of Peace, 88
    mosque, 86—87
    Saint Paul's Cathedral, 89
plantations, 12, 20, 49, 58

plateau, 7, 8
poaching, 57, 60
political instability, 45, 56
political parties, 22, 23, 29, 34
    Democratic Party of Côte
        d'Ivoire, 20
    Ivorian Popular Front, 23, 97
    opposition parties, 30, 31, 32, 43
political structure, 30
    executive power, 30
    judicial power, 30
    legislative power, 30
political upheaval, 22
pollution, 60—61
    water pollution, 56, 60
polygamy, 65, 76
popular foods
    cassava, 126
    eggplant, 126
    hot peppers, 124
    okra, 125
    yams, 125
population, 13, 15, 20, 47, 55, 63, 73
poverty, 11, 45, 46, 58, 59, 77, 109,
    113
presidents
    Félix Houphouët-Boigny, 13, 20,
        21, 27, 64, 87, 88, 121
    Henri Konan-Bédié, 23, 31
    Laurent Gbagbo, 23, 24, 26, 29,
        30, 33, 42, 43, 47, 129
    Robert Gueï, 24, 43

rain forest, 7, 9, 10, 11, 12, 55, 58
rebels, 24, 25, 26, 49, 84
recession, 22, 45, 55, 79
recipes
    kedjenou, 130
    mango fool, 131
reforestation, 12
refugees, 63, 69
religion
    Christianity, 87
    Islam, 84—86
    traditional religions, 89—91
reptiles, 13

rivers, 9, 12

savanna, 7, 8, 10
secular holidays, 121
    New Year's Day, 121
    national day 121
slave trade, 17—18, 69
slums, 77, 78
social customs, 70
social hierachies, 71
social identity, 63
soil erosion, 56
sports, 113—115
    basketball, 113
    golf, 113—114
    rugby, 113
    soccer, 114—115
    softball, 113
    surfing, 114
standard of living, 22, 53, 73, 77
statues, 100
storytelling , 112—113
subsistence farmers , 19, 66
sustainability, 59, 67

temperatures 10
textiles 107—108
timber industry 12
tourism 49—50
toxic waste 60
trading partners 12, 50
traditional festivals 119—121
transitional government 26, 27,
    30, 60

unemployment 73, 77
urbanization 15

wars
    civil war, 24—26
    World War I, 19, 20
    World War II, 20
woman's role, 74—75
writers 109

xenophobia 24